JAMIE GRANT

Selected Poems

CARCANET

First published in Great Britain in 2001 by
Carcanet Press Limited
4th Floor, Conavon Court
12–16 Blackfriars Street
Manchester M3 5BQ

A CIP catalogue record for this book
is available from the British Library

ISBN 1 85754 513 3

The publisher acknowledges financial assistance
from the Arts Council of England

Set in Monotype Garamond by XL Publishing Services, Tiverton
Printed and bound in England by SRP Ltd, Exeter

Contents

Suburb: Anniversary

We've been respectable
two years now; there's
not much left to show, now that
    we've spent the profitable
wedding presents,
and jammed the rest in cupboards.

Home is crimplene country.
The couples jam
the Saturday cinemas,
    gravitate unfailingly
to late-night beers. We breakfast
on blackberry jam and toast.

In summer the garden
sprouted blackberries – the autumn
frosts soon withered them.
    The suburb's a guardian
of public morale. The council's
planted lawns above the sewer.

The Saturday night procession
ends somewhere here, the unmarried
coupling in flats, the respectable
    in orderly progression
discreetly returning
to discreetly separate beds.

Home to crimplene country!
There's a poodle in every garage,
a frock in every cupboard,
    and, if not invariably,
a husband
in every kennel.

We worry over the blackberries'
chances. After these years, still
married! Laminex, cider bottles,
    daisies, tumblers! The country's
laid along its sewers,
the frost assails the kennelled husbands.

Elegy for a Vague Acquaintance

You've achieved immortality
the quick way: a two-column picture
in the *Sun*, with a brief obituary.

Now your face will live forever,
filed and leather bound
in library archives.

For three days, the photo's sprawled
on my floor, staring, almost alive.
You were nobody special to me,

although we watched cricket
together once, stretching out
legs on splintered seats

while sun poured down
as if rain
could never fall again.

You died, a street map
hobbling your knees,
in a car drenched blind

by that cloudburst.
Three days ago.
The rain's still falling,

pushing its fingers down
through the tracks of your grave.
In years to come

scholars will meet you by accident,
mapping a course through dead news
to a thesis.

Perth's Last Total Eclipse of the Sun Happened Over 400 Years Ago

Dampier's *miserable savages*
on the banks of the Swan: for them

each day's business entailed gathering
of fruits and berries, the slaughter

of incautious swans, and then the evening
meal, and a stroll through the twilight

with the family dingo. Four hundred
years ago here, a suburb of bark

sheltered decency, with priorities
not like the present, religion

in stones. Today there's a newsagency
who would have warned of that one day's

unusual event; and a gaudy bottle
shop where their savage descendants

turn to cancel out wretchedness. Above
that ancient, plain domestic life

the abstract wheels described by planets'
   orbits were ready to be

juxtaposed: four hours from dawn the random
   cloud assumed dusk's swan-meat colours.

A brief night followed. People weren't concerned.
   Soon explorers would come.

After the Party, a Walk to the Graveyard

Needing the sea's air the morning after
we scuff new shoes on sandstone tunnels
in the company of tea-tree and wisteria.
You've the instinct of a botanist, and bend
to steal the Government's wildflowers.
Your body ripples like a landscape.

We wind down sand dunes into the burial ground:
where gnats assemble on fresh turned soil
someone has commissioned a marble phallus
to the memory of his wife. Back at the house
they're still reclaiming, workmen with shovels
pursue damp smoke from the billiard room.

We walk on, to the beach. We talk
about your garden, where rows of colour
map out the extent of your civilisation;
your stone hearth funnels smoke
into unknown air, to represent
what you call 'the inquiring mind'.

Shoeless for the beach, your feet are symmetrical
as mussels. The party was no success; the guests
amble to the freeway. Waves have rippled toes
into the sand. You don't wish to think
of death. Out there an empty Coke tin
rides on the menstrual sea.

River Valley, House for Sale

Out on the verandah
I'm leaning into a salt-white breeze.

You stump in musty dark
where mould spills river-green on crumbling boards,

the floors melt at your step,
plaster drips from ceilings crisp as your distaste.

Decided against the place
we look down from the agent's 'charming balcony':

the river spreads below
mould-green tongue under sandstone lips,

boats drift where the valley swerves
for the ocean we cannot think of,

dark water broad as time.
Cold light's patched like rust on the iron river.

Behind us gorge walls split
the sky, black growth against the air's blank sheet,

impassive as a tumour
entering the back of your mind.

The whole valley crumbles.
Salt wind tugs evening across us.

The blackness swells.
We don't know what to say to one another.

Adultery on an Ocean-facing Farm

'These waves of farmland
swell toward their image –
a nape of stone and kelp-
white scrolls where ocean's
paddocks splinter. The ground
is my husband's: his dust-
red possessions arrange
themselves at random
on slopes of edible
green, their complexity
eases my spirit.
The nearest cow eyes
follow us like eyes
in a painting, the soft
heads swivel, chewing.
The land he doesn't own
is that hairless plain we
looked across before,
tufted only by reefs,
its livestock slippery,
intangible: the salt
odour glides in at night
like a shower of rain.
I'm lonely, often.
A she-oak thicket
creases our furthest
paddock. I'll take you
there. The gully's moist,
a notch of shadows, moss
textured, feather-warm. I want
you to be my lover,
I want this transaction
of feelings, elusive,
slippery as fish.
No one shall know about
us. The leaves' meniscus
ripples, splintering
above like a sea.
You can never possess me.'

Snow Holiday with Aunt

The tourist bus lumbers through air-broad fields.

Cattle wade in tufts that graze taut udders,
a man shuffles toward them, dawn's milk soft
shadows stretch from sleep-ploughed eyes, the morning
crowded with light's blunt shapes. The Alps loom
on the mind's horizon, honed edge of snow
between blue foothills and pool-blue sky.
The journey ends at this blade-roofed chalet:
my aunt waits as the driver wrestles luggage,
her face drained like a creek bed, her cheekbones
gaunt as the hills the bus has waded through.
I think of those bone-grey outcrops, ridges
suspending the country's flesh, farm lights glowing
like eyes, ringbarked forests spiny on empty
paddocks.
      Later, I learn of her cancer:
my aunt won't survive the year.
            Next time
I drive there alone. The country's littered
with driftwood tree stumps, dead stone, bone-flat grass.
No cows approach the highway. A tractor
shuffles in sloping distance. Blue foothills,
milk-brown fields. The snowcap sharp as a blade.

Farmer Picking Mushrooms

The idea of emptiness drenches this place
like smoke. Clouds like white slabs of lichen
grip sky's rough hollow bark. I walk in thistle-fur
paddocks. Light slices mottled space.

The cold sun smells of snow – white ledges stain
coarse screes. A long way off, some poplars
grow out of our homestead. No people
anywhere. On hills, sheep anchored like stones.

No need for me to be here. For weeks
these unasked dreams have pushed their roots
down through my sleep. I don't think of my wife.
Coming downhill, I step across a creek.

Now those poplars look nearer. The farm's roof
is thatched with shadows, verandahs pulled
round like a hat brim. Behind, the hills
boil up like clouds. I've found no mushrooms.

Footprints ran through my garden. Her lover's
breath breeds in her lungs like a fungus.

Planes Landing

White metal tubes contain
whole villages: they descend
this steel-white mist, their noise
dazzling to lanes and chimneypots
like a memory of light.

Our hotel's top floor hides in fog
that spreads
across the country like an icecap.
Through double-glass windows
we watch the jets subside

onto pale nets of cobweb hedges,
their slanting tails go down
behind skeleton elms
that hang round the village roofs
like television masts.

Where the hedges intersect
are small vacant fields,
their water green vague as holes
in a fishnet, colours leached
into spider-thick cloud.

We discover we're both thinking
about the crowd of strangers
all gazing straight ahead
down a tunnel of chairs. That's also
the tunnel of self. Their belts click

tight. Sloping down the aisle
discreet as a hostess, sticky
as cobwebs, the same thought nets
each separate mind. Each passenger
imagining death,

muzak spreading like ice.

Sunlight at Montacute (Tasmania)

A gap in mint-smelling trees: their simple trunks
perplexed the complex passions, migrated
from the hedgerows of romanticism,
our ancestors packed on sheep-cluttered decks
with rabbits, pigs and willow cuttings – junk

to multiply in the future's limestone air.
Pale light sifts through moth wings on fence posts.
Lung-deep warrens breathe beneath the stone-
ribbed place he chose to build, my grandmother's
grandfather. In what sense am I his heir?

I study the homestead's ruined shell,
verandahs propped by beams and joists of sun-
light, and strain to conceive of a parson's
reckless son, who'd sail into the void, meaning
to name what he found for a cone-shaped hill;

but instead of his face, I imagine
his latest descendants: my mother's crooked
mouth – expectant as a hare's – and
her mother's fine wrinkled skin like an almond
shell; my own face has two dimensions

only, reversed in mirror silver, worn
by a stranger I can't expect to speak with.
Lava-stone fences. Sheep skulls on hill slopes
of bracken fur. An orchard run to seed,
and willow roots under the rabbit-shorn

garden. Inside the abandoned house, sour clods
of light: the same brilliance curdled on sturdy
farmers, clumsy with muskets hustling
to the gun-slits – ready for genocide.
Believing in self-defence, they'd picture God

bearded like Darwin, smiling *Natural
Selection*. I can't inherit the guilt
of such innocent men, as guilt's an abstract
like blood, replaced throughout the body,
changing in shape all the time; those human skulls

were mashed years back, reduced to bracken-spawn
atoms, fragile moth dust, sun motes. Trying
to explain my visit to these ruins
the simple pretexts vanish like cinders.
In silver light. The bone-shard hill grows white as corn.

Living out of a Suitcase

Now skewers of light
impale the bed.

In the stairwell
a laundry hand

steps quickly on
the fire escape –

and leaves behind only
iron pipes

and stairs, bubbles of paint
on window ledges,

a damp spot
the shape of a sleeve.

Left on the suitcase
an opened letter

explains her altered life:
the house is quite small

but I guess it suits me this way.
The case has joined a queue

of hotel foyers,
diminishing

into the future
like a cone.

Restless traffic outside.
Trace the iron geometry

of pipes – a wall of strangeness
grows behind each

thought. Nothing
to do. Nowhere to go.

*Really, I have to laugh
at myself sometimes.*

Sparrows at the Refinery

City of steel, where no one lives:
tankers wait like empty hotels

on a bored horizon; in what
could be a model forest –

contrived of surgical instruments
and shiny cans – steam grows like trees

from bitter soil, where nothing
is mortal except the sparrows.

Delicate pipes concealing lakes
of fuel: it aches to spread

its poison rainbows. Oil stored
like anger in the heart's cold

cylinder. Some days I conceive
the mind as a place like this,

hostile and intricate, holding
back the fluid bitterness

of language. Vans tow square shapes
out on the highway. Buildings

on headlands shine. Now morning
starts to breathe, a hiss of wind,

combed by electric wires along
the seafront. Inside my mind

the sparrows coldly contemplate
the ground: each thistle-head torso

as particular as love.

How to Fold Army Blankets

Everyone's breath burst out of their mouths
just like the smoke breathed
from the lips of rifles facing the range,

that shattered man-made
hummock whose undigested belly-full
of chollo would one day

stand to baffle archaeology. Each
morning we'd parade
outside the canteen, polished thoughts still wreathed

with figments strange
as dreams. Nights of fitful sleep on sacks of hay.
The mountain peak south

from the camp was blocked neatly as the tall
crown of my old slouch
hat. The days marched on a curve which always

returned to its start;
they finished with the prim geometry
invented to make

soldiers out of children – with heartless
domesticity
which scrubbed, aligned or folded whatever

we weren't expected
to salute. Imprisoned in those ways
we were taught the art

of folding the army's blankets – we'd take
the stitched seam over,
so, and *so*, till it became a flawless

cube of wool, reflected –
in shape at least – in the cold metal pans
they served our meals from.

Remembering that hard-earned skill, a bored
civil servant years
from his army days folded up the map

of Vietnam
the morning we left the camp. His office
must have been spotless,

with calf-bound volumes lined up into squads,
every paper-clip
gleaming. None of us knew a thing about

that room. The frost-smoke
mountains watched us as we started out
on another clear

cold morning. I longed to fold that country
like a rug which we
could stow forever out of mind. No one spoke.

An Auditor Thinks about Female Nature

I have climbed all the way to the summit
of each of those dome-smooth alps, to rest

in whispers of mountain breeze, one hand
braced on the cairn, circled with smaller stones...

The geometric centre of the prairie
is a shallow well which doesn't have

a function. The legends of that place
refer to a giant vine – the roughness

of its bark, the texture of hemp or of cork –
connecting the well to a sky which teemed

perpetual nourishment. Lie down there
and listen to the ground: eons away,

the lava-shifts, the gnash of plates – faint sounds
scratch the eardrum, like the censored thunder

when someone lifts up furniture, in rooms
behind your wall. Sparse transparent glass blades.

The tableland's waste spaces... The City
is located at the junction of two

highways: its suburbs spreading outwards
are shaped into a fan. All my commerce

centres on the harbour. When the vessels
go there, they soon unload their cargo, their

hard prows nudging into a salt-slick wharf.
Sometimes the storms upstream can dye the river

scarlet – the colour of house bricks, of sandstone...
On the other side of the mountains, there

is said to be another city. Rumours
of its influence have reached the provinces

where pragmatism rules our way of thinking.
Its produce, they say, is called Art. I tried,

once, to imagine the form of its gaudy
turrets, the ornamental ponds, the groves

of statuary; but the room inside
my head remained unfurnished, its walls as blank

as the lined sheets in life's stern ledger book.

Rainbow

The family's new Humber was speeding
    through the country along the road
to Sydney: no other car could pass us
    as our father stepped on the gas
like Donald Campbell, whose life was reading
    matter for the cramped back-seat load.
All of us jeered whenever Pegasus
    loomed above the scarlet canvas
awnings of a garage, in the small towns
    he throttled back for – the petrol
company our daring chauffeur worked for
    was symbolised by a scallop.
Under the sun the grass was blistered brown,
    and gum trees looked like broccoli
disposed at random in paddocks; far
    from the highway a horse galloped
out of a sun shower, without taking
    wing. Wide shafts and narrower tubes
of light were propped against a sky crowded
    with textures – near the horizon

a monster cauliflower was making
   a rainbow's bright palette describe
a curve which landed next to a cow shed.
   Mother was authority on
such matters: it was then I learned about
   the crock of gold that was buried
beside the already-receding shed.
   Surely we had to stop and dig
it up? None of us was old enough to doubt
   the truth of our mother's words.
But nothing was done. The gold receded,
   and soon gold sun was standing
all around us. The only thing we'd gained
   was disappointment. The black road
kept on vanishing under the Humber.
   I thought about the ways we could
have spent it, then wondered how the rainbow
   caused the gold. Ways I could number.
'Our' brand of petrol was the best because
   our father said it was, and who
had any reason to think otherwise

when nothing one's parents said could be untrue?

Ants in the Shower Recess

Tiny black-skinned warriors,
   the aboriginal inhabitants

of this suburb do not require
   a land-rights movement, having not

moved from it. The modest cuisine
   of the coloniser (that's who

I am) fuels their factories:
    the soldiers carry head-sized

sugar boulders, and crumbs bigger
    than loaves, back underground; their ranks

marching through the kitchen look like
    columns of refugees.

The scouts they dispatched to my shower
    have found some of yesterday's

personality, washed up in
    the grouting. Their scientists proved

it edible: why not devour
    Gulliver? And now they're waiting.

One day the daily monsoons
    will not happen; the mountain-range

of food-ore will rest from earthquakes.
    Then they can send the miners;

I will be excavated, with ants
    like a chain of firemen passing buckets

to each other, when their one thought
    comes about – all of my skin

become a crowded market-place,
    my picked-clean skull swarming

with more ideas than ever
    it contained before, except

that every one is this one idea.

Jumbo Jet

The black-and-white television
in the laundromat airs a repeat
of *McHale's Navy*. An iron
that man is pressing on his trouser pleats
    produces a rhythmless click, as if
a log-fire were set in the other
    room. Beside the dryer the whiff
of gas is overpowering – smothered,
    I step back to where its window
resembles a porthole on an aircraft
    carrier, except that the view
is of clothes, which vault over each other, deft
    as a squad of acrobats. Most
of the washing tubs are empty, their lids
    propped open the way the posters
lean outside the newsagency. Threads
    and scraps of lint are islands
on a floor of ocean-grey linoleum,
    or flaws on an ocean of sand-
beige . . . it hardly matters; the machine hums
    and the television mutters
to no one. Just to help pass the time,
    I go outside again – it's better
in the open air. An alarm clock chimes
    in some house down the street. At first
there's a vague background murmur, no louder
    than a simmering pan, increased
at once until it's the sound of a downpour
    of rain; a vacuum-cleaner whine
swells into an ambulance siren note,
    roaring like a bushfire – and then
the jet's in sight, seeming almost to float
    in a space among the rooftops.
Its nose, derived from a dolphin's, reflects
    a rivet-point of light; its wing-flaps
hang ajar; engines depend from brackets
    close to its torso, that's newly
painted. The man with the iron has stopped
    using it now; he walks past with unruly
hair, and yawns, going into the betting shop.

Invasion of the Jellyfish

This morning's tide delivered jellyfish
into the bay, a vast
suspended cargo

in the sheltered inlet – where fishing boats
wait anchored, and there beside
the rowing club, under the bridge,

at the entrance to the canal, and here
in the shallows, hindering
wind-surfers; they're a forest

under water, in which dwarfed fish wander
confused, like cattle
strayed from their pasture. Each one

of the jellyfish has a different size,
and yet their form remains constant:
a pink rubber canopy

above what appears a knot of soil-bound
roots, attached with fine plastic
tubes. They are house plants removed

for re-potting, covered over with mauve lace,
delicate silk brocade tea-cosies.
They are parachutes bulging

in a liquid breeze; umbrellas closing
then opening; water-filled tampons.
They are uprooted mushrooms –

ideograms of nuclear explosion;
or they'd be the domes
and cupolas at the Kremlin,

except for those caps of glossy vinyl,
like some modern stadium
built to house the Olympics.

Returning from my walk, I find the tide
has retreated, leaving one of them
stranded on the boat-ramp,

deflated like a used-up condom: it's reduced
to a smear of jam, found in the kitchen
after somebody's nightmare.

Deathbed

As a result of some trivial slight
my great-aunt went to bed in disappointment
and remained there for thirty years, the length
of the rest of her life. She claimed to feel
unwell, though physicians could bring to light
not one symptom of physical ailment.
Because she would not exercise the strength
to cook or to sit at table, her meals
were always prepared by expensive
caterers – from her room, which was upstairs,
she'd let an empty hamper on a rope
down to the neglected garden.
Delivery men knew she was alive
as the consignments were no longer there
on their return, though the velveteen drapes,
above, did not show who awaited the burden.
When a dinner had not been touched, one time,
the courier went to tell the police
after a number of days: a sergeant broke
through the door, and found, instead of a corpse,
my great-aunt jammed tight in her bath, supine,
nude, and comically immense. Twice
I was made to stand at the foot of her oak-
panelled four-post bed, where I felt both bored
and afraid. The house was the cause of my fear,
its locked-up rooms and creaking corridors,

and the flour-sweet musk in the bedroom.
The adult conversation washed around
me, of scarce interest to any child's ear,
till I went on the forbidden verandah
looking over the violent jungle blooms
which smothered the back of the house. The ground
looked far away, and quite as frightening
as the ghosts I had persuaded myself
to imagine, in the airless hall
downstairs, where dust-sheets cloaked the furniture.
Through the trees there came a blink of lightning.
As I suffered from indifferent health,
my worst dreams involved sickness, making all
the more nightmare-like the disease conjured
from nowhere by the creature in bed
just behind me. A thunderstorm was moving
on the harbour, its cloud draped like a curtain
in some nineteenth-century parlour.
At that time my terror was reserved
for things no one else could see, and nothing
was as fearful, it seemed, as this woman
alive on a deathbed; her mind's death-green pallor.

Still Life with Desks

Dust-yellow light slants
all over the city,
a new coat of paint
for the upper stories;

it lies across sports-fields
in narrow lanes, the aisles
of a floodlit, cold
pavilion. Tiles

on the imitation
church spires of take-away
chicken operations
deflect the neon-bright rays

which scatter among
oil-slicks on the river,
and cling to the long
stems of fever-

coloured aniseed plants
on the railway's
stony embankments.
The train has been delayed

near the end of its journey,
the city centre's wedge
of oblong forms, that vary
in height like the ridge-

line graphs at the stock
exchange. We're up close
to one high-rise block,
watching its precipice

of glass blink back even
more light than the polished
leaves on a eucalypt. Then
a square-edged

shadow moves up the side
of the building, like
a rising water-level. Lights
turn on inside

as offices submerge.
Windows, losing
their blankness, emerge
to frame a painting:

Still Life With Desks
And Clerks; another becomes
a television set,
screening some Board Room

Drama. The woman
sitting opposite
jerks awake: the train
has begun to pull out

from the shade. The light
touches her ankle,
that's swelled-up in the heat,
and prickly with stubble.

How Old Are You? –
Three Poems about my Cousin

I. DAYLIGHT MOON

'Genius is next to madness,' said my mother,
'and your cousin is the living proof.' The talent
which provoked this much-used maxim was a bent
for arithmetic: in any decade after
the 1950s, we would have compared his mind
to a computer, but then computers remained

to be invented. Intricate multiplications
and long-divisions were performed in his head,
promptly and accurately, as if he had
long been prepared for each calculation,
a matchless party trick, wasted in a person
who was not invited to parties by reason

of madness. His condition was no shameful
family secret, but a source of anecdote
and wry group-humour – it amused us to quote
the latest findings from his search for fanciful
place-names in the Sydney street-directory,
one of the two volumes in his library,

the other being Melbourne's telephone book. Rhyme
appealed to him, and alliteration,
but the purpose of all his investigation
was specific: he was in quest of the sublime
music of numbers. 'What is map seventy-two,
D-4?' he'd ask, his voice a swift staccato

monotone, like the speech of a teller-machine,
knowing the answer was always *Lillli Pilli*,
his favourite suburb for its rhyme with *silly*.
'Christopher Codrington,' he'd continue, '16
Seventh St Sptswd.' Mostly his conversation
consisted of abrupt interrogation

compelling a numerical reply: 'How old
are you? What do you weigh? How tall? What year
were you born?' His gift could not be used in a career
just because he would always do what he was told
should not be done. The life he endured instead
was that of a prisoner. His parents were dead;

he hardly noticed, held in institutions
from the age of five. The specially assembled
family he had sprung from might have resembled
a closed-off hospital ward, into which, once
in a while, he was released, to a shower of names.
The asylum – we supposed – was the same

as a boarding-school, only more severe.
Whatever he suffered there must be deserved,
as his actions were deliberate and perverse:
this was my mother's view, one not founded on sheer
cruelty, only on the age's innocence.
It was far too late for my cousin, when science

identified autism. He was called a lunatic,
for all that the full moon's influence on the brain
had been disproved. Ignorance can generate pain,
though knowledge is often as cruel to eccentrics,
and on purpose. In our parents' gravel driveway
an unfamiliar car would announce the day

of his visit: he'd wander round the house,
shuffling in oversize boots like a pensioner,
half-stunned with motion-stunting tranquilliser,
his expression a bare-gummed grimace. He'd drowse
and then wake up, in a cushion-plumped living room
which had been stripped of every breakable heirloom

before he came. A pebble-shaped daylight moon hung
above my father's lawn, a left-over Christmas
decoration, suspended near an isthmus
of cloud in the picture-window; his brother's damaged son
held court in the lounge, greeting everyone he knew
with a robot-voice question: 'How old are you?'

2. THE HOSPITAL BELL-TOWER

Dimpled still water, like cellulite thighs:
        here, a floating buoy –
a word Americans pronounce to rhyme
with 'hooey' – resembles a baseball some boy
has struck out of the park. It lies
among the hulls of a fishing fleet, which at this time

in the day remain immobile as a herd
        of grazing livestock.
The trawler nearest the shore is attached
to its twin, a ship that won't ever see dock:
were a photograph to preserve
the replication, each of its halves would be matched

like a Rorschach test – you'd recognise there
          the wings of a bird
constructed by engineers. Another
more morbid suggestion might have occurred
to those inmates whose minds compare
every two-sided place to the focus of mother-

hood, a doubled plimsoll-line becoming
          the pink folded lips
of a blood-gorged imagined vagina.
The people exist, for whom such visions eclipse
all daily reason: their numbing
imaginings are flamboyant as household china.

They're found in the asylum my cousin
          was sent to for years
before his mother heard about the beatings.
The nineteenth-century bell-tower which rears
up over this fishing haven
belongs to the same institution. Since meeting

the new terminology, its clients
          are disadvantaged,
not insane. My aunt died, leaving her son
an orphan, incapable and middle-aged,
with an adult intelligence
confined to a cell in his brain, to which no one

could unfasten the lock. Is the key
          lost in the harbour,
in sight of the sandstone tower, beside
its gardens and its rose-fringed arbour
where men in dressing-gowns are free
to borrow the air? A bell chimes out. Resting on the tide

the trawler also rests upon its double,
          to which the name-plate,
reversed, is shivering in the way a horse
twitches off flies in afternoon's moist heat.
A cormorant stirs, to trouble
the high-gloss surface: unfurling wings like oars,

it sets out on a clumsy march across
    the water, making
flap-wristed arm-gestures – an entrant
in a Bird-man rally – before taking
a smooth longer stride, to recess
its undercarriage, and skim above the white shirt-front

of its mirror-replica, transformed
    into a bomber
gliding unseen for the dam. The short flight
punctures the stillness like a comma:
the image-boats have not reformed
when the waterbird chooses a rail where it alights.

3. CHRISTOPHER CODRINGTON

Reading a specialised work on the history
of the Caribbean, I encountered a name
to take away my breath: in the 17th century
the Governor of the Leeward Islands
was Christopher Codrington, the grand-
son of a wealthy namesake preceding him in fame.

For my family, that name bore a different
resonance, as it was the one which enchanted
our retarded cousin, in the course of his frequent
excursions into the telephone book.
Somehow, those repeated consonants took
hold in his mind, becoming part of his curious chanted

repertoire. Governor Codrington established
a theological college in Barbados,
by means of bequest, in a will which furnished
his successful ancestor's plantation
for the purposes of education,
'doing good to men's souls' – 'and 300 negroes

at least always kept there, and a convenient
number of Professors'. In the book's description
of the college I found something reminiscent –
the 'balustrades looking over lawns,
pediments doubling themselves at dawn
in the fish-fluttering lake' – these were a prescription

to restore the deeds of my long-dead grandmother's
mansion to the vacant possession of mind.
Though I never saw him as a child, the bother
left after that cousin haunted her house
as a ghost. His presence was the cause
of the chicken-wire which was stretched across the fish-pond:

on a previous visit, he had attempted
to drown a baby – another cousin – among
the carp and lily-pads. His assault was prompted
not by malice, but by a spirit
of experiment; in the same pursuit
he unscrewed every light-bulb in the building

to conceal them in a cupboard. He liked to break
household objects, clocks, bells, or bottle-openers,
dismantling mechanisms with all the care it would take
for repairers to reverse the damage.
There was no way for anyone to gauge
his exact intent. Did he mean to create offence,

or did he merely suppose his madman's humour
was shared by his relatives? There was calculation,
surely, when, sitting in our grandmother's parlour
soon after she reached the age of eighty-
five, he asked that dignified lady
how old her mother had been when she died. Information

was not the point of the request, as he knew
in advance the answer was eighty-*four*. 'And how old
are you?' came next. Another time 'Granny, do you
masturbate?' was his opening remark:
we envisaged him at once in a park
with his trousers unfastened, and all the room turned cold.

In the name of Christopher Codrington
our cousin gained an obsession at least equal
with his passion for figures. From irritating
his own family members, he began
to persecute an innocent man.
It would have remained a story lacking a sequel

except the law of coincidence dictated
that I had met the victim, who went to the school
I did, although some years before – to that hated
place, imprisoning as an asylum.
Drugged to pre-empt his worst tantrum,
our cousin was allowed to come out for tea, with our cruel

reluctant limb of the family tree
which stood in his brain as clear as a courtyard oak
existing only when seen by Bishop Berkeley.
When he vanished from the room, someone
had to pursue: he was on the phone,
breathing 'Christopher Codrington? How old are you?' Joke

or not, the unfortunate Codrington was forced
to move, and now there are no Codringtons at all
in the directory, their surname being cursed
with an unknowable enemy
whose purpose could not be explained any
more than it might be prevented. At Codrington Hall

in Barbados there are robed postulants who fill
the shady corridors and library, at least
300 of them – students, not slaves. The lake still
echoes stone lintels. Someone questioned
our cousin concerning his passion,
to discover 'Christopher Codrington is a priest':

another mystery; the Codrington at my school
became a stockbroker. In more recent times
a State regulation invited ridicule
by enforcing the discharge of cases
like that of my cousin from the places
which had sheltered them for decades and more. Such schemes

are known to the jargon as 'community care',
though their object is not care but economy.
Warned of his release, our cousin was struck with fear:
he had grown content with hospital
routine, and now he faced the terrible
fact of normality. The news alarmed his family,

but rules are rules. He was placed in a boarding house
in a district which refugees from the Second
World War are obliged to share with the refuse
of society: a suburb of strudels
and bratwurst, and of cast-away needles.
My youngest brother, who is always family-minded,

compelled me to sample the atmosphere of this
hostel; he took me on a dutiful visit.
Our cousin was led to the gate, folding both his
wrists limply over his breastbone – the paws
of a kangaroo, or dinosaur.
His belly loomed as large as a pregnancy, as if it

were grafted in place by unnatural means.
Two misshapen teeth jutted from his lower jaw
like the sad stained molars on a ruminant beast.
Yet he was clean and well dressed. He knew
me at once, and exclaimed 'How old are you?'
'You tell me how old I am,' I replied – this was four

days after my thirty-ninth birthday. He snapped back
'Thirty-nine. Does Christopher Codrington masturbate?'
Next day I had a reason to be on the block,
nearby, that is renowned for its cake shops
– for its slice of Vienna, perhaps –
when I noticed my cousin coming along the street

in my direction. I crossed the road to watch him
before he looked around. He did not seem to be
a misfit in this place, nor even a victim,
compared to those with port bottles
under the palm trees, whose spittle
dangles from chins like shattered cobweb. Methodically

he was looking over the cakes. At each window
he paused to ponder the display of Black Forest
cream-cake, of madeleine biscuit, and marshmallow
slab, of pastry daubed in a glaze
like a brand-new car. The air of his gaze
resembled any idle window-shopper, whose interest

was intent but not in focus. He might have been
an eccentric professor of divinity,
on this street, in exile from the Caribbean,
or a Polish mathematician,
condemned to a menial position,
who had just resolved the problem of infinity.

Powerhouse

Equal in size to a rich man's manor,
the powerhouse which overlooks
the cove is now disused. There is no planner,

yet, who seeks to transform its framework
into a department store. The building
is of bare grey cement, and a winter

day's sour-milk sunlight is gilding
its flank. Random as a carpenter's
workshop, the weed-bristled grounds. On the roof

a row of smoke-stacks, like the funnels
of the *Titanic*. There are waterproof
plastic sheets and sawn-off planks, fennel-

hedged iron sheds among dunes of coal
– these could be filled-up ashtrays – and skips
which lie abandoned, like beached rowing shells;

there's a water-tank, on which a faucet drips,
that is stained with rust like a face
disfigured with birthmark. The powerhouse

itself resembles the crankcase
of a tractor left out in the meadows;
it is also a vacant temple,

whose divinity, long since repealed,
consisted in engines more powerful
than any proven act of the revealed

true God. Like most gods, the machines became
obsolete. Beside this promontory
the harbour water has the polished gleam

of the benchtop in someone's newly
installed dream-kitchen; on it, a single-scull
moves like a water-strider, discarding

a trail of expansive double circles.
Each print is transient as an insect's wing.
In the lee of the power station

the rower pauses a while, holding his oars
dead-level, as if in contemplation,
while the boat becomes a perfect wooden cross.

Description of a Fig-leaf

Mashed globes of fruit, in the shadow
of the Moreton Bay fig tree: at first they seem
to be droppings of an unknown
small animal. The tree's roots buckle and seam

the asphalt footpath, that's wearing
its mud-pack of berries – a cosmetic
preparation. Other roots, tearing
the soil, twine over each other, elastic

as those sinews on the forearm
of a plumber, who strains against his spanner;
and more roots take their form
in mid-air, hanging down tassels in the manner

of an elephant's tail. The tree
itself has the skin of an ageing circus
elephant, and its canopy
of leaves is the size of a marquee. Curious

about this plant? Then take away
a leaf: one side of it is glazed as a piece
of enamel; reversed, it stays
dull matte; its size is not so great as to suffice

for the inventors of modest
style, the evicted tenants of Eden, as it's less
than a bikini, and just
the same as a cow's ear, being a milk purse

of sap. Now consider the way
the leaf presents geography. Its glossy
side's deep green slopes impersonate the play
of light along a valley

somewhere in feudal Asia: there's a channel
for irrigation dividing
its paddy-fields into opposing panels,
and each field is provided

with a vein that's a smaller ditch. Beside one
there appears a bomb-crater,
not burst, as might be thought, by Americans,
but by the invading Aphid.

Turned over, the leaf is a fish, or at least
it's the skeletal remains
of a sturdy central spine, increased
by ribs like wing-struts – fine bones

to catch the throat. Looked at from a distance
the tree's convex structure is most
like a chandelier, for its wax-skinned figs which dance
and glow in the sun – a host

of lighted candles. The ruff of green lace
beneath them is made up of leaves
in equal abundance – it would seem, for a space –
to those fish beneath the waves

the exact size of a fig leaf, and equal
in number to the valleys with
a leaf's form, centripetal,
that exist on the surface of the Earth.

War Planes

The green-tweed fields were chequered as the bad-taste
trousers of a comedian, or a golf
professional; a freeway made a vast

zip-fastener which divided them in half.
Its ellipsis of white-painted hyphens
streamed under the car, as I drove myself

past statues smothered in lichen,
the roadside shrines of North Italy.
Some jets raced over, hissing like syphons,

presumably headed for Tripoli,
the town in those headlines I couldn't quite
understand. For springtime, it was bitterly

cold. The horizon's mountains – the same height,
it seemed, as a church spire – wore a fringe
of snow, which in places had trapped the light

to resemble a scoop of blancmange.
Along the freeway, a processional
of military transport came in range,

decked in breeze-twisted official
regalia. Grapevines covered in nets
knelt by the road, as if for the confessional,

before a green-robed poplar, and willow-thickets
nearby followed the course of a stream
where a plaster-walled farmhouse was set;

and this landscape seemed a terrible dream
of the longed-for holocaust, from which one
would wake in a sweat. Could a tower of steam

have arisen in the heart of Milan
within so short a time? Looming above
the orchards and distant villages, a column

too brown to be cloud, bulbous as a clove
at its peak, moulded itself in the shape
of a massive woodland toadstool. I drove

toward the cloud, as there was no escape
if this was what it appeared, while reason
deflected itself to recollect the gape

of tourists in a nave before a vision
of St John. Although an unbeliever,
in that church I'd had an impression

of being allowed to relive a
Gospel miracle, as the blindness imposed
by contrast healed from my sun-dazed retina.

I had stumbled on a tableau composed
of living supplicants, some nuns and black-
robed worshippers, crouched down as if posed

as bird-watchers. Suspended over their backs
were the noiseless bubbles of prayer
cartoonists might imagine: these were cracked

by my arrival, and by the entry there
of a man in chequered trousers who strode
up to the altar, blandly unaware

of actual devotions. His voice, loud
vowelled German, echoed in the transept,
a noise enough to alter any mood

of reverence. And I had to accept
myself as such a tourist, scarcely less
intrusive, as gingerly I stepped

along a narrow side-aisle, where stained glass
furnished an alcove in scenes of blood-drenched
martyrdom. A sculpted marble carcass

was lying on what seemed like a bench.
The tortured figure of Christ, the skulls
and skeletons, the painted faces wrenched

in gruesome suffering, froze my pulse,
then, with their comfortless implication
that God had been nothing else

than Death personified. For this, nations
had grown, and overwhelmed each other; for this
they had cowed populations

with the promise of an abstract bliss
in exchange for approved behaviour,
a truce which includes an abyss

of logic at its centre. The power
in the human mind to envision
eternity reduces to a vapour

when confronted with the simple question
What happens after that? Apocalypse,
the answer proposed in Revelations,

is left in just such an eclipse
on the morning of the Second Coming;
and thus we complete an ellipse

in the process of reasoning.
The dread of ceased existence, which attends
every mind aware of its own being,

can't avoid being counter-balanced
by a terror far more subtle,
of a possible life without end.

A paradox can have no rebuttal;
and yet some architect possessed belief
enough to order the stone-built marvel

where I discovered this bas-relief
depicting the fate of the damned. While modern
secular thinking excludes an after-life,

I recalled my own childhood notion
of one's entry into Heaven, involving
a waiting-room – some church-sized cavern –

where people stood in lines beneath revolving
fans. You had to fill out the right forms,
supplied by a faceless clerk, absolving

yourself of the world. The place I had formed
this idea was in the vestibule
of an infirmary, where the First Form

had to queue, our first day at boarding school,
on the way to a medical check-up.
By then, all that had been learned was the rules;

a perpetual gas-flame flickered
beyond the cypresses, at my father's
oil refinery – it had not occurred

to me, at that age of ignorance, to ask whether
he owned that grotesque mechanical
fairground, if we were as poor as my mother

always complained. I was not practical.
My health was delicate. I was lazy,
said all my reports. Metaphysical

thoughts careened around my brain, both crazy
and rational, propelled by gales of fear.
The sea-fogs hung around all day, a haze

like ivy on the buildings, while the school year
unfurled itself. I did not want to die
in a war, much less if it were nuclear,

and yet I built model war-planes. The sky
was a thoroughfare for planes from the base
beyond the lagoon, and the jets would fly

over with the roar of a hellish furnace –
though Hell was beyond my belief, despite
my acceptance of Heaven. Not a place,

but a state, we were told, by the polite
evasive chaplain. This was not, for me,
enough: I wanted something definite

on the mechanics of infinity.
Neither teachers nor books ever supplied
such knowledge, so I had a theory,

misconstrued out of science class, which applied
the structure of the atom to the whole
universe. What became of us when we died

was a complete alteration of scale.
By some unspecified process – my scheme
lacked logistical detail – the soul

resumed its existence at an extreme
of matter, where atoms were galaxies
or planets mere electrons. It would seem

from my ill-informed reading of Mee's
cyclopedia that our next level
of being could cause our size to increase

till the Earth was only a particle
within an atom formed by the Solar
System. On Sundays, the junior Oval

was a runway for model aircraft, where
their single-stroke engines made a buzz
like an amplified fly. The circular

flight of each model, controlled by its fuzz-
cheeked owner, was directed by hand-held
cables – the painted balsa-wood Spitfires

were out on missions, each of which revolved
around a fixed position, as planets
orbiting the sun, or as protons held

in an atom. It was no less than at
such times, than in every morning's Chapel,
that mortality would come to rivet

my attention. Yet I wasn't unhappy,
until the newspapers filled with the Bay
of Pigs, and then for some time I grappled

with the fear-fuelled conviction that the day
of reckoning was already at hand.
Cuba's crisis seemed no further away

than our Sydney holiday home. I planned
how to shelter from the Russian atom
bomb, which I thought would be certain to land

on the refinery. Meanwhile, at home,
my father was practising golf. The world,
the prophets had forecast, was due to come

to an ultimate combustion which hurled
us to nothingness – but now was too soon
to be fair. My theories tipped and swirled,

confirmed and denied at once, by the one
instance. A hurricane roared in my sleep,
but next day the sand-spit and lagoon

lay calm beside the shore. I had to sweep
the passage outside my dormitory,
where a dust-mote storm aroused my eyes to weep:

a sunbeam encompassed a galaxy,
sloping from the window like a buttress
on a cathedral's wall. In Italy,

over two decades later, I thought of this
in the precincts of the same cathedral
which inflamed intellectual distress

in the sensitive spirit of Stendhal.
When the tourists had left, I too returned.
to the light spilling over the portal

in clay-coloured Florence, light which had burned
on Petrarch, and on the swarthy waiter
who married my former wife. Lessons learned

out of school are those remembered later.
The forecourt cobblestones, beneath the tiled
dome, bore a cluster of demonstrators,

repeating angrily the much-reviled
name of Reagan, idealists who protest
too much, like the whining of a child.

With intentions which are mostly the best,
the belated followers of Gandhi
invite scepticism only from the rest

of those who may well incline to agree,
as the anger comes to look rehearsed,
in chants repeated by rote, like Sunday-

school prayer recitations. Now the worst
had come about, I saw, in the shadow
of the Cloud, and those prophets had been cursed

with bitter fulfilment. Its mushroom billow
was nearer to the car, a Grimm beanstalk
higher than all Manhattan. A fellow

human must have started this, after talk
had changed a bluff into a precipice –
a fellow only doing his work,

a soldier or nuclear physicist,
who was also still a boy like myself,
with a model at last ready to test

in the open air. All of the world's wealth
would have no value, soon. Approached, the cloud
showed its profile, solid as a rock-shelf.

The country which surrounded the road
was replaced by a factory now.
Instead of the shrines, there loomed a billboard.

Power pylons stood in a field, with a cow.
In a land where for centuries people
had harvested their gardens and bean-rows

the fires would consume every staple,
as well as those fruitless commodities,
Art and Faith. Then, punctured by a steeple,

the cloud began to weep, its identity
as a spring storm abruptly revealed.
The rain came with such an intensity

that a spectre seemed to walk in that field.
My alarm, being false, had been a waste,
yet it felt as if a contract had been sealed.

Skywriting

Cool, clear autumn morning, so still
the knock of someone hammering
a nail rebounds from the floor
of the valley, with its shimmering

metal rivulets: that shadowy
vale in fact is a railway yard.
For some reason, on a Sunday,
a jet pilot has expelled a hard

stream of smoke behind his aircraft,
so precisely outlined
it could almost be a steel rail.
It's chilly, and there's no sigh of wind.

Flying high and fast, the pilot
has drawn a straight line, an arrow
of exhaust from one horizon
to the other, a path whose narrow

course is seen from the ground as curved,
so that it appears an enormous
basket-handle has been attached
to the land. Unlike the mischievous

Air Force trainee who, in the skies
over Perth, etched out in smoke form
his own private parts, as if he were
a vandal on a railway platform,

this pilot has not diverted
himself, leaving a colourless
rainbow arched over the city
and over those suburban palaces

secured by the Bank. A rainbow,
though, is never as wide an arc
as the flowery canopy stretched
there now, like an archway in the park

arranged for a wedding. Beneath
its bridal bower, an airliner
coming in low resembles
a clumsy groom, cutting it finer

than he should, arrived with buttons
unfastened. An unhappy man
in Melbourne years ago rented
a skywriter, in desperation,

to advertise for a wife: people
always look at the sky. The track
made by this morning's jet may be
a less intricate message, yet its lack

is not of import: its simple
curve is the curve of the face
of the world, and hence it implies
all things within its embrace.

Like the world, the smoke meridian decays
before your eyes. Out of vision
an engine roar persists, sounding
like a far-distant storm's reverberation,

and like the football crowd I heard
once in a garden, a commotion
which could only be accounted for
as the shimmering pulse of the ocean.

Mushrooms after Rain

Rain echoes in the light-well,
the clatter from a pool

of typists. Easing, its sound
is the fountain

which plays in the chrome-rail
quiet of a hotel

foyer, where business deals
are made. Grey half-light, for days.

Trees show through
a veil, as though

on a TV screen with blurred reception.
Every lawn in town

has grown unkempt,
acquiring the cheap

lank hairstyle of
unemployed youth.

Sun stays a memory.
Forgotten machinery

spawns fungus-textured rust.
When at last

we awake
to a dawn of vacant

sky, the effect is that of turning
to an unprinted

page, unaccountably,
in the daily

newspaper, as if those lines
of rain

were once set
in type. In the streets the wet

has scrawled its signature,
according to its nature,

on sheets of uncreased
concrete, water squeezed

out of stone. A drain has fixed a plaque
over half

the bay, so its mud-and-granite
hue seems a potter's

glaze. And mushrooms
have bloomed

overnight, in
a multitude of imitation,

innocent and sinister.
Beneath a power

pole, they have taken on the form
of a Nazi storm-

trooper's helmet, while
their white

bald orbs
on the golf course

offer far down
the fairway an hallucination

of hope.
Or else they are clean headstones

in a military graveyard;
discards

of a china factory; new-laid birds' eggs;
human sex

organs. Where the boathouse
casts

its square pool
of shadow, there are toadstools

arranged like restaurant tables
on a fashionable

outdoor terrace. I once
lived in a house

where mushrooms
invaded the bathroom:

indestructible,
they levered tiles from the wall

like prisoners
making an escape – or, rather,

like illegal migrants
whose means of admittance

outflanks
authority. Their rank

scent tainted the air,
and yet there

was something of the beautiful
in those skulls,

freckled
and coated with velvet,

and in the fleshy black pleats
furled in underneath

which spilled an ink-
like powder over the sink,

the dust of regeneration.
Having to clean

this stuff
one could not think enough

of its heedless will
to survival;

it was hard to deny
a life-wish like my

own, strong
as a beating

heart. Scrubbing was in vain
as they would return

ahead of mould
and mildew. Everything spoiled

in that climate.
Mist sat

on the river
as close to its contour

as fungus
ledged on a tree-trunk.

There were saucer-
sized mushrooms in the horse-

paddock. My wife
got a fungal growth

on one lung, which the doctor
mistook for a cancer,

a counterfeit tumour
resolved to a harmless rumour

only in surgery.
It seemed a mystery,

as sourceless as the rain
which began to fall again.

His Nibs

Round-boled, the eucalyptus tree
puts one in mind of a stout worthy

burgher – the Lord Mayor in his robes,
perhaps, slyly addressed as 'His Nibs',

half-dressed before a pageant, and half
in disarray. Its peeling bark ruff

looks like a skin complaint, a collar
of loosening flakes, at once the colour

of rust, and stone, and of flesh – except
the papery scabs are incorrupt.

Beneath its insect-nibbled cloak, stitched
to resemble the intricate patched

surface on a geologist's maps
of the Outback, a white torso slips

in view, owning a sleek complexion
like a woman's before the invention

of the cancerous pastime, sun-bath.
Its limbs, the means through which a tree draws breath,

embark at the level of a man's
skull to pursue divergent plans,

as water running downhill seeks out ways
without resistance – and yet their maze

flows upward, feeding on nourishment
of light. Its end is embellishment:

a shiny peruke of downward-hung
leaf-silk, an oil-textured shantung

in pale green, comprising foliage
almost grassblade-slender. At each stage

of growth, the trunk has added a ring
as if there were someone honouring

its worth in new-struck chains of office;
but jewel-red sap-stains compromise

such honour, leaking from joints and seams
in the cream-bland integument. Dreams

reinvent these lurid sap-trails
as welling shotgun-pellet holes

in the unlucky corpse who revealed
the graft of His Nibs, lying in a field.

Mysteries

All that is solid melts into air, wrote
Karl Marx, whose tomb I visited,
though not on pilgrimage. A crooked stone,
nearby, marked the final descent of the
first Englishman to be killed in a fall
from a hot-air balloon. Marx looked for all

the world like a wealthy capitalist,
frozen there on his marble plinth. The air
itself was melted snow, that day, a wet
mist which soaked through umbrellas into your
hair. The tour-guide, a history
student, took a route through the cemetery

which involved a search for memorials
of last century's murder victims, and
for others whose ends were exceptional.
A crypt with a padlock on a rust-stained
gate encircled the bones of the woman
who sunk *The Well of Loneliness*. Sun

whitened tiles on a distant rooftop, but
its effect was of frosting on a baked
Alaska cake. With some hindsight, I thought,
the statue of Marx had rather looked
more like a watch-and-waistcoat vicar,
a bearded evangelical preacher,

standing on an upturned box to campaign
for salvation – and it's true salvation
of a kind was his concern. Endless rain
made a shroud for that complaining nation
I had flown to from a summer which burned
still in my absence. Memory returned

me to Highgate more than a year after that,
in another summer, on a walk
around the cove which opens Sydney out
as a diorama. This was near dusk,
and thunderclouds seemed built as solid ramparts
at each point of the horizon's compass:

they were made of air, and yet they seemed
like stone, the imitation battlements
on a vulgar mausoleum. Becalmed
in equal lanes of angled light, the yachts
and speedboats of our local bourgeoisie
were set on water smooth as the glossy

concourse at the prestige motor dealers,
while fishing craft stood in for the working
class. The boats were lined up to give the feel
of racing cars on a Grand Prix starting
grid, all headed in the one direction,
and the rear-winch and derrick construction

of trawlers let them be those tow-trucks
which follow like ambulances. To note
the resemblance would, if someone had asked,
please me less than it ought, as it seemed that
day nothing could show me contentment.
Without any cause for resentment

I felt unease, and felt the more so while
it was unprovoked. The clouds, I observed,
were like shapes half-remembered from dreams, whole
images swollen and faded in absurd
surrealism, like the melting ice-sculptures
in Japan. One cloud seemed to own the features

of a schoolmaster who sought to humble
me one time – but it quickly dissolved
and became a horse's tail. A rumble
of thunder rounded the shore of the cove.
Over the mountains, the sun had vanished
into a cloud which was like a burnished

copper cooking pot, with a luminous
rim. Unhappiness lacking any clear
source, as unbounded and out of focus
as English mist, is an emotion near
to being universal, yet no one
is comforted to know this, and none

can prevent its occurrence. Another
cloud was poised above the level rooftops
in a suburb where apartment blocks cluster
as a man-made peninsula, and drapes
of rain hung limply from its stone-coloured
lintel; part of that distant shower had

trapped the sun's rays to create what looked like
a sloping concrete ramp. Advertising
some brewery, an airship seemed to glide
across that slope as if it were moving
itself to a different dimension
– the way, that is, an actor steps from the screen

in the untrue cinema of your dreams.
My habit has always been to suppress
melancholia, as to share it seems
an imposition; nevertheless
Freudians tell us any repression
is damaging – that to give expression

to every nameless fear is the way
to confound it. Psychoanalysts grow
rich on terrors of people who will pay
to relive painful nightmares; even so,
the heart remains as much a mystery
as next week's climate. Something feathery

detached itself from a cliff of sandstone
cumulus. Saving the needless expense
of analysis, some women telephone
their friends to exorcise life's discontents,
and yet all those who expel depression
in such talk seem none the happier, on

the whole, than those others who are hoarders
of pain. Each cure is as mysterious
as disease. Walking by twilit waters
I reflected on people's various
tempers and needs. Before me the mountain-
sized towers of the city's central wen

in shadow seemed no more than a series
of fence poles, propped in a timber-merchant's
yard. And then there was something curious:
first it looked as if another airship
was gliding over the smokestacks at the
power station, and then it seemed to me

a saucer-like object was hovering
there. Made out of a silvery metal,
it had a form as of two domestic
dishes joined together. It seemed brittle,
and yet its edges were defined clearly
against a backdrop-curtain of pearly

storm-clouds. Jung produced a book on Flying
Saucers, but reckoned them symptomatic
rather than true. As I kept on watching
credulity rampaged in a panic
down the solemn cloisters of the mind
– until the slightest breathing-out of wind

made the metallic dishes stretch and stream,
and resolve into a strip of cirrus
illuminated by a single beam
focused on it by the setting sun. Thus,
I thought, are fantasies constructed
in which whole families are abducted

by alien beings; momentary
conviction swept me, as if I had solved
a baffling universal mystery.
That's a solution for the self-deceived,
of course. It did not explain the lack
inside the heart which generates these black

troughs of feeling, deep as the depressions
on a weather chart. No one understands
– entirely – human motivation:
that is why the most ingenious plans
of idealists and economic seers
cannot succeed. To recognise our fears

and animal hungers is nowhere near
enough. That beam of sunlight, now, chose
one of the buildings in the city's square
of fence-post timbers, and made its windows
glow, as if it had a skin of pure gold
like the towers in the Samarkand of old,

or like the golden towers in Manhattan
built by Asian dictators, which survive
their architects just as things which happen
in dreams remain to haunt our waking lives.
Nightmares melt away, as do all solids,
and all that's melted billows up as clouds.

A Good Deed

The red-whiskered bulbul
had come to build a nest
in the vines which conceal
the bathroom pipe's descent

beside our kitchen door.
Its chat would distract us
from breakfast, and from our
papers, in which the news

was all about a war
over distant deserts.
If anyone went near
the nest, the bird flapped its

protest with the bluster
of a politician.
A fine scarlet whisker
made the bulbul's jawline

seem adorned with a scar, while
another square of red,
patched on below its white
waist, evoked a leathered

pair of Bavarian
trousers. The feather crest
surmounting an avian
hairpiece gave completeness

to a suit of finery.
The nest was the same size
as the china coffee
mug under which the day's

headlines were pinned down. One
morning I looked inside
and saw there were two eggs, brown
and camouflage-freckled

on a mattress of straw.
Yet the bird's subterfuge
failed, as the nest, too low
on the vine for refuge

from marauders, could have
been overrun by force
at any time. To give
it protection, I thought,

could be my day's good deed,
so I kept watch over
it. No more than a week
or so had passed before

the eggs transformed themselves
into two beaks which screamed
reflexively: bivalves
fixed to flower stems seemed

to strain out from that cup
of twigs and feathers. For
a few days they grew up
contentedly secure

under surveillance meant
to be no less benign
than the kind government
of a near-divine

Enlightenment monarch.
But then I peered around
to find one of the batch
had fallen to the ground

where a gaping scallop
mouth continued to plead
for food. I had to help,
of course; it took no great

effort just to replace
it in the nest. Meanwhile
the nestling's parents raced
about, their voices shrill

with concern. Like music
the language of birds
has beauty and rhythmic
structure, but, lacking words,

has no apparent
content. Human vanity
took its course: what was meant,
I assumed, was a cry

of gratitude for that
one action of simple
charity; it could not
have been, for example,

a cry meaning distress.
I left the nest alone
for another week. The success
of the operation

seemed not to be in question,
for the birds had resumed
their shrill distraction
near the door. The rescued

prodigal child remained
safe in the nest. But then
I thought to make sure, and,
if only to know when

the infant bird acquired
an adult's uniform, checked
on the nest. It appeared
that the nestling was dead:

there lay a stiff cluster
of damp-textured feathers
devoid of the lustre
worn by living creatures.

The other one was gone.
I had dropped the carcass
into the compost bin
when I thought its heart was

beating still, as the chest
was writhing urgently.
I reached for it at first
before coming to see

the nature of my error:
it was only alive
with maggots. The horror
passed as quickly as if

it were one of those scenes
of slaughtered soldiery
shown on our TV screens.
The maggots were very

clean, and looked like teardrops
or pearls, all unaware
any other life should stop
once they were in the air.

Ballade of the Unhappy Golfer

He hangs his head as if some dredge
    of recollection had withdrawn
a misery long past; the sedge
    and marshes where he wanders spawn
    tough-whiskered reeds which sigh like corn
and look to him at least as tall
    as pylons, while his partners scorn
the golfer who has lost his ball.

If only he had used a wedge
    or had not pressed with all his brawn
it could be resting on the edge
    beside the fairway's silky lawn:
    instead it's deep amongst the thorn
and seems to be beyond recall.
    He wishes he had not been born,
the golfer who has lost his ball.

You've seen a funeral cortège
    and felt the sadness of the horn
which keens beyond the cypress hedge
    to end the services at dawn;
    you may have heard of the love lorn,
those swains who yearn to end it all,
    but none of them are more forlorn
than golfers who have lost their ball.

Envoi

    Caddy, I simply could have sworn
we'd find it where we saw it fall.
    It's very rude of you to yawn
when I have lost another ball.

Helpless

Foghorns on the harbour;
dogs in the street;
tomcats; a circular
saw; the robot bleat

from a burglar alarm;
some cockatoos;
other birds one can't name,
as well as crows;

opera recordings
the neighbour plays;
and all the minor things
which in the days

we'll never see again
were background noise
one scarcely noticed when
they pricked the poise

of routine calm like pins:
now each of them
focuses and sharpens
the senses, then

lets us breathe out once more.
The occupant
of space which was, before
one day's event

to spare, is slumbering
peacefully still.
While we are numbering
the time until

our new-born daughter wakes
a squall of rain,
like an ocean wave, breaks
on the windowpane.

The world and all its sounds
remain unchanged
and yet the very grounds
are rearranged

on which our lives are led.
No more can we
collapse upon the bed
except when she

has ceased from the discord
which fills the air
whenever she is bored
or just aware

that there might be a lapse
in our concern.
The sound of dripping taps,
a leaking urn,

and further irritants
which used to grate
with chalkboard dissonance
now aggravate

us for a differing
reason – they each
suggest a quivering
repeated screech

which could be the distress
of a small child.
Lying prone and helpless,
trapped like a wild

animal in a cage,
or a tortoise
upside down, in her rage
she's at a loss

for words, though one could not
of course mistake
her meaning. From her cot
she aims to make

the long convalescence
of infancy
a time when her parents
will constantly

attend on her summons.
As we listen
there goes an ambulance;
or it isn't ...

The Conversations

The smell of barbecues in the sunlight.
A formation of racing cyclists,
like an eerie squadron whose noiseless flight
creates a cold sensation which persists
long after they pass. A middle-aged woman
in walking shoes exclaims to another
dressed as she is: 'He bought my affection;
he *bought* it.' She could be someone's mother.
Birds on the grass like a fungal disease.
Splintered beams of light among the trees.

At the car park there's a post-and-rail fence
where a florid-faced man, who is clearly
a drinker, has taken pains to balance
an empty bottle on each post, nearly
a dozen in all. And then he climbs up
on the fence and walks its length, teetering
dangerously as each leg sways out to keep
from upsetting a bottle, metering
his progress like a drunk forced to walk a
white line. Could he have been a tightrope-walker?

A girl replies to a muffled question:
'Most', and her interrogator laughs. They
are walking by the lake where reflections
of their surroundings seem, on this still day,
to multiply the brightness surfaces
hold: a palm-crowned island glows with a green
more intense for the glimmering nearness
of its duplicate on water. Obscene-
looking carp hover beneath that sheer grain,
like half-submerged thoughts at work in the brain.

There are tree-trunks with mildew which has grown
overnight; it looks as it would if brushed
on in luminous paint, reminding one
of the moonlit clouds last night, which rushed
above the house, then paused as the wind died,
seeming for a time like a scene-painter's
backdrop, daubed with the same brand of dye.
Passing, a bow-legged woman in rainbow-
patterned tights tells her friend: 'I couldn't take
it any more, you know.' Soon the calm must break.

Digging Machine

The Water Board was digging up our street,
so that for weeks it looked as though
one of those rocket-powered missiles, heat-
seeking, computer-controlled, had flown

here to gouge a man-deep trench, in an act
of senseless war. The destruction
wrought on kerbs and flowerbeds was, in fact,
achieved by a few construction

workers, most of whom stood about to watch
while the youngest of them wielded
a truck-sized digging machine with the touch
of a billiards player. Shielded

by our cherry tree, I joined the audience.
The machine had the yawning jaw
of a hippopotamus, the presence
of a yellow-scaled dinosaur,

and, folded on its back, a scorpion's
tail. Or so it seemed. In practice
that trailing limb could be both a weapon
and a tool used with the finesse

of surgical tongs. The wide mouth had scraped
up rubble from the road surface,
browsing a silt-choked riverbed, and gaped
with appetite, before the service

of the sting was called for. It then attacked.
The layer of bedrock concealed
beneath the concrete was easily hacked
away – a hot blade through congealed

grease – exposing pipes deep in the ground, rust-
caked like sunken treasure-casks.
The machine raised up these iron hulks just
as primly as somebody asked

to sip tea from expensive porcelain:
the terrible blade which could cut
through stone might also take hold of a grain
if required. The young man who sat

on its leather office chair held levers
taut in both hands as if playing
a video game, his lips pressed together
in a focus that could be saying

This is an art form. All that had been built
in this scene, with the destruction,
was the product of pure human skill.
Crows watched, hoping for carrion.

Lunch with my cousin the would-be actress,
in a bar on First Avenue, New York.
It was Labor Day, and the President
had decreed that American righteousness
should be celebrated with a work
of performance art, whereby residents

would link hands in a chain stretched over the land.
As visitors, my cousin and I could see
the irony: all her friends were cocaine
users, while the room I was renting, and
soon returning to, was owned by three
lesbians, and shared with cockroach chains

stretching all over the floor. There'd been nights
when I had woken to sense a wire-thick
feeler exploring my face. The house was
in Brooklyn, wooden, three storeys in height,
towering above a geometric
plain of disused basketball courts. Gang wars

had raged over these spaces, now fenced-off
and scrawled on by weeds. One mid afternoon
a brand-new Porsche was parked outside the door;
as I passed it I heard a kind of cough,
and saw that its driver had a teaspoon
and a shirt sleeve rolled in readiness for

a needle in the arm. All night sirens
wailed. The lesbians upstairs were never
in sight; they were holding group therapy
sessions for damaged women. No silence
lasted long, in that place, if it ever
occurred, though the people there seemed happy.

If this could be the end of the earth,
it was also its centre, or at least
as near to it as anywhere. The decay
which surrounded me had a kind of worth
in that it showed depravity at its worst
could still be endured, and sometimes a ray

of hope would light those ruined tenements:
for example, there on the fire escape
of a building deep in grime, overlaid
with spray-paint hieroglyphs, crude and intense,
someone had taken the trouble to create
a bonsai garden. The longer I stayed

acclimatising there, the more it seemed
less dangerous and grim. I passed the days
riding the subway to those parts of town
where threat receded, and where marble gleamed
in light-filled galleries; in bright cafés
where smiling waiters carefully wrote down

what they were told, harmless and insincere;
in gardens and plazas where musicians played;
and beneath the colonnades of each famed
museum. On Labor Day it was clear
that my cousin had things to do, so I paid
for my share of lunch, and, leaving, aimed

to walk home. I had noticed that the bridge
which raised the subway trains briefly out of
their tunnels had a causeway where people
could be seen, cycling or on foot: a vantage
point above most of Brooklyn, and above
the broad East River. High as a steeple,

the Williamsburg Bridge was slowly rotting
away, but it ended close to the part
of town I had been staying in for weeks.
There were places where the causeway's slatting
had gaps like broken teeth, but still the art
of its design was evident, unique

and heritage-worthy. As my ascent
of the causeway began, a festival
feeling seemed to reign. There were family
groups coming down, and brightly-dressed girls went
by, calling out, one on a bicycle.
There was only a minor anomaly:

as I neared the highest point of the climb
a pair of pasty-faced fellows stared hard
at me as they passed, and nodded to each
other. They both wore T-shirts smeared with grime
and lightweight running shoes, and I heard
one of them grunt, but as I was in reach

of home there seemed little cause for concern.
At mid-bridge, I leaned on the parapet
to see the river's acres spread below,
the type of panorama one can earn
through mountain climbing. Level as a carpet,
it was fringed with apartment blocks and low-

roofed warehouses, all of them diminished
by height, and specked in a houndstooth pattern
with white speedboat wakes. The boats themselves
were scarcely visible. A seaplane finished
its descent, taxiing into Manhattan
like a yacht, while the buildings' stacked-up shelves

seemed prepared for an onrush of shoppers;
the sun was bright as neon. The shoreline
and the air seethed with action: those buzzing
flies I could hear were some helicopters
which circled over Brooklyn's supine
corpse. Satisfied that there could be nothing

more to see, I set off again, and glanced
back as I did, noticing those grime-smeared
men both wheel around, a hundred yards
away, to follow me. They had no chance,
I thought, of catching up. The causeway veered
to the right some way ahead, then turned hard

73

left to slope down towards an underpass.
The left turn, though, transformed the atmosphere.
The happy families and laughing girls
were left behind. Rubble and broken glass,
powdered on the path, glinted in the air.
And now it was quiet. Smoke poured in curls

from a distant building site. I could run,
of course, but might not doing so announce
the weakness of one in need of succour?
Perhaps it would be wiser to go on
looking unconcerned. An eerie silence,
now. No footfall, no ... GET DOWN, MOTHERFUCKER!

Both of my arms had been seized, and a voice
roared in my ear, loud as a rock singer
or a sergeant-major. A hand held a knife
the length of a baking dish: I'd no choice
but to submit. Something like a finger-
nail made a dent in my neck. So my life

is ending today, I found that my mind
observed: at once, I was perfectly calm,
and thinking, This is unexpected.
Approaching, it seemed, my death, I was resigned
and mildly curious. Gripping my arms
as they searched me, their expressions reflected

in a blade, my assailants were the ones
who seemed afraid. They kept on screaming
while time slowed down for me: soon I'd have stepped
out of it, to watch the inconvenience
my death would cause. As if I were dreaming,
or else half-conscious, having overslept,

I thought of people having to disperse
my books, which towered like apartment blocks
in a room where dust motes rode the angled
sunlight. Then it was over. A last curse,
and they fled, light footed as before; and clocks
resumed their purpose. I disentangled

myself, and rose, exhilarated,
and began at once to run in giant strides
like someone on the moon. Earth's gravity
could hardly hold me down. Unrelated
thoughts flew about in my mind, and collided
with each other. I'd never felt so free.

The mood sustained me to the deadlocked door
I put the world behind, and then it fled
on rubber-padded feet. The safe, barred room
was filled with fright. New from the hardware store,
the mirror-blade knife seemed almost to loom
again before my eyes, saying: Soon you'll be dead.

Lives of Men

Toothless, wizened, and bald,
unable to walk,
or to make what is called
'meaningful talk',

my four-month-old new son
appears, like all men
when their lives have just begun,
as he will at the end.

The Woman in Black

A day of high wind and rain in the park;
　　and then the sun breaks through,
stilling the air as though an unseen hand
　　had turned a switch in the dark.
　The sky's left with remnants of blue
whereon loose heaps of cloud resemble the sand

and sawdust piles on the floor of a house
　　which is being restored.
Joggers come out, in their tight-fitting clothes.
　　A woman in a blouse
　strides past as if she can't afford
to waste time. Poisonous green algal growths

and lilies bloom on the lake. The light
　　changes again, a mood
darkening the whole of a crowded room.
　　From nowhere, a haunting sight
　appears: wrapped in an attitude
of straight-backed calm, and all in black, there looms

a lace-veiled woman who twitches the reins
　　of a smart pony trap
out of last century. She has the look
　　of a Spaniard whose veins
　course with noble blood. With a tap
from a cane-handled whip, fixed to a hook

by her side, she urges her dark horse on.
　　More joggers pass: a short
man in a hat, and a tall one whose forearms
　　revolve in the motion
　of a swimmer. Elsewhere, the sport
is football: on a field fringed with palms

the players in clashing colours divide
then merge in fractured
patternings, a faulty kaleidoscope;
their cries fill the air's wide
echo chamber. The unstructured
sky now has stray clouds the colour of soap.

Then one of the joggers, an older man
with grey hair and a red
complexion, stops, seizes his chest, and falls
down backwards, slower than
a tree limb that is struck dead.
People run for help, too late, with hoarse calls

which sound like the footballers' cries. And there
is the woman in black
again, in her varnished cart like a bier,
with her long shiny hair
hanging loosely over her back,
quite detached, as she glides away from here.

A Human Soul

The scientists say the human soul
does not exist; yet they expect
us to believe in a black hole

their instruments cannot detect.
The reason for their rigid faith
in something which cannot reflect

light or heat; which is not beneath
or far above; which can't be felt
or touched – a theoretic wraith

– is mathematics. The star belt
wherein this hole may be, or mayn't,
stretches like a leopard's pelt

across the sky, a spill of paint
onto a darkly polished floor.
One does not have to be a saint

to have a faith that there is more
in our existence than the things
our eyes and ears take in: the door

of reason is not closed; it swings
to let in falsehoods in disguise
as well as truths borne up by wings.

Watching a new-born baby's eyes
open to accept the world, who'll
still be sure our souls are lies?

The Valley Murders

I.

We walked all day, the three of us, over the farms
which lie between the foothills and the weir. A hot
day, for September, nearing the end of our terms
at the school among the mountains. Though it was not
a strenuous route, the countryside we walked through
was mainly waterless – wide paddocks leached a dusty
green – with pinetree clusters making garlands for the few
red farmhouse rooftops that we passed. There were rusty
ploughs lying about in the grass, and rust-coloured
cattle in groups like foreign tourists. It was strange,
for me, to be in such company, moist-collared
and silent, as we headed for the blue hunched range

on the horizon. My companions were not friends
of mine, so we were less than a well-met threesome.
I was the smallest and weakest, the one who ends
up trailing behind when rucksack-burdened climbs come
at the end of day. There was also a loner,
a strongly built boy with an alliterative
name, cryptic and unpredictable, the owner
of the sharpest Swiss Army knife whichever I've
seen. And the third member was our headmaster's son:
to grow close to him was to invite suspicion,
though he was agreeable enough in person;
his life was limited by the derision
of others for those who are thought too close to power.
Now the sheds and windbreaks of another homestead
were coming into view. As it had been an hour
since we last sat down, and since our canteens had bled
dry, we pressed the brawny Henry Harte to approach
its kitchen door, to have our water containers
filled afresh. He returned not with a reproach
but with the farmer's wife, and tea to sustain a
long afternoon, and with hot scones, and jam, and cream:
these were the 1960s, the last decade
before the presence of strangers would come to seem
something to fear – the decade which planted the seed
for much later trouble. We walked on then, over
the open fields, passing more sombre-faced cattle,
and, once, a plantation of rifle barrel poplar
trees whose shadows were rungs along the blank metal
of a road. The length of those stretched-out shadows meant
that soon we would have to choose a place to sleep
with wood to fuel a cooking fire, and pitch our tents.
The field beside the road was overrun by sheep,
but it was not far to a farmhouse with a barn
which crouched beside it at the end of a cypress grove.
If we camped among the trees we would do no harm,
so we went to see that the owner would approve
our choice of camp site. Gerald, the headmaster's son,
was sent to the door, as we judged his manner best
adapted to the purpose, and he came back soon
with a wiry, smiling man who welcomed the rest
of us, and offered up the shelter of the barn
for the night, on condition that we help to clean
it out next day. 'Come over to the house for a yarn

when you're set up,' he added. We could not have been
more pleased to find such hospitality: a dread
of being alone in each other's company
weighed down our thoughts. A high-roofed corrugated shed,
the barn was a surprise; it was filled with debris
of a quite unlikely kind, not aromatic
litter of cows and spilled machine oil, but shards
of human life: clothing, age-destroyed elastic,
and heaped-up books and documents, old playing cards,
and letters – in opened envelopes – lay scattered
in there. We'd have a bonfire the next day, having found
out which of these long-treasured items mattered
and which did not. In the meantime, though, we were bound
to visit the farmer's house. We left our packs
in the barn, and made our way to his garden gate.
A storm could be seen coming over the stooped backs
of the mountain ranges. It was not yet too late
for the last of light to glow in the cypress tops.
On the rose-bordered garden path there came a noise
of thunder like muffled gunfire; in bulbous drops
the rain began, as the farmer called 'Come in, boys.'
He was on the phone in the hall, so we waited,
overhearing stray fragments of speech which were soon
to add up: 'No, I'm not getting agitated,'
we heard him say. Then he came back into the room
looking concerned. 'I've got some trouble with a cow,'
he explained. 'The vet can't come until eight-thirty
tonight, and I might need some help from you boys. How
would you like to stay for dinner? It's a dirty
night, by the looks.' We had no chance of debating
whether to accept this offer, as Henry Harte
had said that we'd be pleased, without hesitating.
So the farmer showed us into another part
of the house, a dining room with furniture
which might have been unchanged for fifty years, except that
a mahogany radio set made the culture
of the present intrude on one corner. We sat
down, and listened for a while to some results
from the Tokyo Olympics: Gerald was a sports-
man, though Henry Harte said that proper adults
did not indulge in games. Any uneasy thoughts
were soon dispelled, as the kindly farmer returned
to introduce his wife. She was just as wiry

as her husband, and her temper could be discerned
from a twinkle in her eye. Polite enquiry
ensued, as to our health, and then the meal was served,
great slabs of blood-red beef on willow-pattern plates.
While we ate, the farmer had remained reserved,
his mien being that of one who anticipates
some large event. One of the cows which were in calf,
it seemed, was having a difficult birth. Our task
would be to help the local vet, on whose behalf
our work would be unpaid – it was not much to ask,
to save the unborn calf. The rain was roaring, now,
on the farm's iron roof, with a sound like a train
in a tunnel, but we set out to find the cow
as soon as the vet arrived. We went with a chain
and a torch into the pouring darkness, wearing
tarpaulins and hats. The cow looked like a boulder
in the torchlight, lying on its side, despairing
eyes turned towards us. It was about to shoulder
a deeper agony. The vet was talking while
his stethoscope shifted from one place to the next
on the wet flank. 'It's a bad sign that she's down. I'll
do what I can for her, but the calf … ' A short, vexed
silence. 'It's already too late.' A second tail
protruded from the cow, a small tasselled bullwhip,
as well as a touching cloven hoof. 'Now, if they'll
assist,' he said, referring to us, 'I'll just slip
a rope round the calf and we'll try to drag him out '
The rain had eased by now, and the moon showed through gaps
in the clouds. A strange tug-of-war was thus about
to take place, with one side a corpse. 'Ready, then, chaps?'
said the vet. 'Now *heave*.' But the dead calf was stuck fast.
We pulled until our hands were burning with the strain
before the vet gave up. 'It looks,' he said at last,
'as though we'll need the cheese-cutter, here.' To sustain
his strength, he took a draught from a flask, then replaced
it in his bag, and next got out a piece of wire
with handles at each end, giving us a foretaste
of its use by plucking at it, making a higher
note as he tightened its length. There were more spaces
in the clouds, now, and the scene was drenched in moonlight.
Stripped to the waist, the vet reached his arms to places
in the cow that we thought inconceivable. 'Right,'
he said, at length, as he gave the wire a last twist,

and his blood-streaked hands emerged into the eerie
light, and he began to saw. Handles in each fist,
he worked like someone pumping out a nearly
dry well, and the rasping noise we heard was the wire
cutting bone. Stooped over, varnished in gore, intent
and deliberate, the man seemed a tableau of dire
extremity. Yet it was in a light which meant
that it was not quite real, like something in a book,
or in the black and white which reduces horror
to a kind of abstraction. The vet only took
a minute or two before tautness in the wire
relaxed, and it fell away. We took up the rope
again, and hauled on the severed half – *Heave, Henry
Harte*; the hempen halyard's hardness held out faint hope
for the hapless Hereford (that week's poetry
class had been the Anglo Saxons). And then the legs
and tail emerged, glistening with slime in the dim
half light, cut off at the waist. The other part next.
The vet did this on his own, pulling out the slim
useless torso, and the head with its unopened eyes.
The drama was all over. The cow would survive,
the vet thought. We did not feel that we'd earned a prize,
but now as we watched the vet's station wagon drive
out the gate, the farmer offered us coffee
before we went to sleep. It was close to midnight,
but none of us were tired. 'I'll tell you a story,'
he added. All at once, his care-creased eyes seemed bright.

2.

His wife had gone to bed. We sat down in the room
where, not so long before, we had faced those portions
of dissected beef. Like a return to the womb,
or to the scene of a crime, this recollection
was briefly disconcerting. But now the farmer
commenced his story with a question. 'Have you heard,'
he asked us, 'about the Wonnangatta Murders?'
We knew of the place, at least – that sweet-sounding word
referred to a valley deep among the mountains
shown on our hiking map. One had only to read
the titles on that map to sense that the terrain
it covered was harsh. Upon it the watersheds

82

of three great rivers were marked; there were also
jagged heights whose very names conveyed an air
of threat: The Razor and The Viking were two
peaks jutting like rock-bound islands near Mount Despair,
and the tide-worn reef which leaned toward them was known
as The Crosscut Saw. This was joined, in turn, to the dome
of Mount Howitt, as round and bald as the skull bone
of the dignitary it was named for, and home
only to eagles. At the other end of the row
was Mount Buggery, the schoolboy's delight, whose slopes
tipped steeply down into The Terrible Hollow.
It seemed that the map told a story of ruined hopes
and grim events, and yet Wonnangatta Valley
was said to be a kind of paradise, its green
and tranquil flats closed off from the world. A volley
of raindrops clattered on the roof outside. 'It's been,'
the farmer went on, 'more than forty-five years since
the murders, but people here still don't like to talk.
The valley's a beautiful place. I went there once,
myself, but it's tough to get in. You have to walk.
It's walled in on three of its sides by the mountains;
the fourth is a gorge on the river, with rapids
no one can cross. A spur off the Howitt High Plains
leads into it, but that spur's so steep it forbids
even horses from taking it, let alone carts.
There's also a mountain pass over from Grant,
which was how the Bryces came to be in those parts.
At first, old Bryce, with an American immigrant
called Oliver Smith, was working at the goldfields.
Grant was a gold town, then – this was last century
– though it's deserted now. Smith and Bryce saw the yields
decline, and decided to head for the valley
to start a cattle station. Both men were married,
and Bryce had seven children: the first time they crossed
the mountains the two youngest of them were carried
in gin cases strapped on each side of a packhorse.'
At the mention of gin, there came a stifled snort
out of Henry Harte, but the farmer continued
his story. 'Bryce and Smith were partners for a short
time only, before the first tragedy ensued,
when Ellen Smith died giving birth to stillborn twins.
Their graves are kept, still, in the valley, near the old
homestead, under a stand of pines – "All without sins",

the wooden marker reads. After another cold
winter, Smith sold his share to Bryce and left for good.
The Bryces stayed on. For more than twenty years, they made
an agreeable living, having plenty of wood
for building material and fires, hens which laid
and cattle for meat and milk, while the river flowed
close by the homestead, with speckled trout in its pools,
tame enough to tickle. The absence of a road
connecting with the world of churches, shops and schools
left them unconcerned. As the children grew up, they
moved away, although some of them did not go far:
there are Bryces in the Mansfield district to this day.
Old Bryce died in nineteen-two, and when the Great War
began, Annie, his widow, died too. The family
then sold the place to Geoff Ritchie, another name
this district still knows well, a grazier wealthy
enough not to occupy his newly bought claim.
Instead he went and hired a manager to run
the property – a widower named James Barclay
was installed. A fellow suited by isolation,
he was an expert bushman, who lived happily
in the timber farmhouse built there by the Bryces,
until after a few years he found that the work
was too much for a man on his own, a crisis
resolved when he employed John Bamford as his cook
and odd-job man. Bamford was a fifty-year-old
with a murky past, but because the war was on
Barclay had no choice. If all that he had been told
could be believed, he had taken on a person
one should approach warily: there was a rumour
that Bamford had strangled his wife, although nothing
had been proved. He was known to be of ill-humour,
and his temper had drawn him into fights, often
enough over trifles. But then there were also
rumours about Barclay, as he well knew, and which
he found easy to disregard. On his say so
he was a loner; he'd reply, "That's a bit rich",
if anyone mentioned the death of his young wife
from tuberculosis; she was only eighteen,
while Barclay had been in his forties. Her short life
sharpened his urge for solitude, into a keen
blade. His neighbour and only friend was Harry Smith,
stepson of Oliver, the pioneer, who lived

further down the river, beyond the gorge and cliffs
which enclose the valley. Travelling there still involved
a hard day on horseback. The Great War, by this time,
was three years old, and New Year was approaching. Ten
days before Christmas Eve, Bamford made the long climb
into the valley to start his new employment,
and after eight more days James Barclay and his cook
rode over the mountains to Talbotville to vote
in the Referendum. People thought, by the look
of things, that "the two were getting on well", to quote
a police report. They stayed overnight at a
hotel in the gold town, which was why, on the same
day, when Harry Smith rode into Wonnangatta
Station, he found no one around. He'd claim,
later, that he felt he was being watched. He left,
and did not return for three more weeks. The new year
was a fortnight old when he found the place bereft
and still deserted, except for Barclay's dog near
the stockyard, looking half-starved. Smith raised the alarm
in Talbotville, and came back with a search party.
For several days they scoured the hill-shadowed farm
until someone found the rotting corpse of Barclay.
His head had been cut off, and it lay some distance
from the partly buried torso; its expression
was one of mild surprise. There was clear evidence
of what is called "foul play", despite the condition
of the decomposed remains. A bullet was lodged
deep in the spine. Bamford was nowhere to be seen,
alive or dead, nor was his horse, so it was judged
at once that he was the murderer. Had he been
disturbed, the search party wondered, while still at work
on Barclay's half-completed grave? Now the police
were called, and the hunt for Bamford began. It took
several days for word to reach the head office
in Melbourne, two hundred miles away, but at last
a detective was sent to examine the scene
of the murder. He and a pair of troopers passed
through Talbotville and Grant, all on horseback, a lean
and purposeful threesome, with their grizzled chest-length
beards and cabbage-tree hats, each wearing a three-piece
suit despite the heat. The detective's pipe was clenched
between his teeth, and the horses stumbled to their knees
on the steep defile which led into the valley.

And then they arrived in that cool and sheltered place.
Cattle stood around on the flats, grazing peacefully;
some knelt down by the river, which was clear as glass.
The homestead's red metal roof and wide verandah
could be glimpsed through a screen of cypresses, beneath
a forest-clad hillside. Tempted to meander
through that seeming innocence, they were short of breath
for a time, and after their ride they were both tired
and starved. They entered the kitchen as soon as they
got to the farmhouse, and found all that was required
for a hearty meal of bacon, eggs and tea.
The house was undisturbed, as if it awaited,
still, someone's return. The kitchen had been scrubbed clean,
and the table laid with knives and forks, and shakers
for pepper and salt on either side of a fine
hand-made vase. The troopers shook pepper thickly
onto their eggs, and prepared to devour the spread;
but their food was turning a vivid and sickly
colour. The pepper had been strychnine. Was Bamford
a poisoner as well? was the question. There still
was no sign of him. Another search brought no more
clues, though they combed the sheds and the stockyard as well
as the house; they had raked over the four
graves under the pinetrees before they gave it up.
Winter was closing in, by now, on the mountains
and the High Plains, so the detective's return trip
to Melbourne was perilous and harsh. That explains,
perhaps, the mistakes which were made, over the next
nine months. The newspapers printed an artist's sketch
of Bamford, amid the floridly phrased context
of a reporter's second-hand account, while each
police station across the state posted Bamford
as "Wanted for Murder". The case drew quite a deal
of attention. Hundreds of strangers came forward
with information, but little of it was real.
In Sandringham, a beachside suburb of Melbourne,
a man identified himself as John Bamford
to the police, and was held in the cells for seven
days, under a constant guard, until someone heard
from the next suburb's station that the same fellow
had, several months before, announced that he was
Jesus Christ. Meanwhile, more than ten feet's depth of snow
covered the Howitt Plains: it had been a fierce,

long winter. The snows lingered there all through the spring.
The war was over, and normal life was restored
to the farms and sawmill settlements which still bring
this district its living. People could now afford
to give thought to their future. The goldmining towns
were occupied by ghosts. In early December
a young cattleman crossing the Howitt High Plains
settled for the night at Howitt Hut. Remember
that steep spur out of Wonnangatta? Well, the hut
is situated not far from where it arrives
at the crest of the range. Constructed of slabs cut
from the dense mountain-ash rainforest which still thrives
on the nearby slopes, it has a hearth and chimney
made of stone, and a pile of logs for firewood leans
against its back wall. Anyone who wants can stay
in these huts, which are often found on the high plains
and in the mountain country, on the condition
that they cut more firewood to replace whatever
has been used. At this time, Bamford was still missing.
It was a night much like tonight: brief but severe,
a storm came over Mount Howitt, and then it cleared
enough for the moon to shine its coach-lamp between
galloping clouds. The flicker of a fire had cheered
the cattleman while the downpour fell like a screen
across the doorway, but now it was burning low.
He went outside to fetch another log. The moon
picked out his surroundings with a pure, limpid glow
like that of a gas-light; a winter afternoon
would be this bright, he told himself while walking round
the hut. And then he saw the figure of John Bamford
standing beside the woodpile, pointing with one hand.
He did not move, and nor did he utter a word.
A cloud erased the moon for just a moment,
so that its light was doused, and when it drenched the scene
a short time later the pointing man was gone. Bent
limbs of worm-white snowgums gleamed. What this sight could
mean the young man guessed: he began to shift the woodpile.
The work took him an hour in the fitful moonlight,
and at the end of it he had solved the futile
search for the absent Bamford, whose body was right
there, beneath the woodpile. It had been well-preserved
by the snows, and the bullet-wound in his temple
seemed fresh and horrible. So he had not deserved

to be the murder suspect. It all seemed simple,
now. Bamford had witnessed the murder, and had been
observed in his turn. Imagine the grim pursuit
which came then, as Bamford fled headlong up the mean
spur's screes, the murderer behind him, both on foot,
scrambling over rockfalls, or through bracken thickets
and stands of tree-fern. Climbing up onto the range
must have taken most of a day, in the waistcoats
and hobnailed workboots of the time; the last exchange
between the killer and his second victim would
have been at night. Bamford got as far as Howitt
Hut, and he may have thought he was safe; or he could
have been too tired to go on, as he was not fit
enough to outrun the other man. A single
bullet ended it all; and a summer squall blew
out of an empty sky. Scraping the shingle-
stony soil with bare hands, the murderer soon knew
that he could not dig Bamford's grave; he intended
to build a pyre instead – there were signs that a fire
had been set at the base of the woodpile – then did
his best to make it seem that the cook had dire
designs on his employer, going down the spur
again, and straight to the homestead kitchen. He stole
Bamford's horse after he had placed the poison where
it might be incriminating. And on the whole
he succeeded. To this day the murders remain
unsolved, and I doubt that he'd be charged, any more,
if the police ever found enough proof to gain
a warrant ...' We had listened in silence, so far,
but now Gerald interrupted: 'Are you saying
the killer is still alive?' The farmer nodded.
'And you know who it is?' 'All of us are staying
quiet, but everyone round here knows who did
the deed. The police knew, as well, but what, now, can
they do? Three of them went to Howitt Hut, guided
by Harry Smith, to bring the body back to town.
Coming from Mansfield, it was a hard three-day ride,
but the return journey was much worse. They had slung
poor Bamford over a packhorse saddle, but soon
he began to thaw. The smell was like a well-hung
side of mutton, as alluring as a hormone
to the dingoes, which harried the troupe as they rode
through the bush, leaping to take bites of that cargo.

On the second night, unseasonally, it snowed
among the peaks, and the sky's archipelago
of cloud was full of foreboding. All through the night
they heard the dingoes' howling echoed from the steep
canyon-like hills which surrounded their camp-site.
It became too much for them. There was no deep
need to give Bamford a funeral, so they just
abandoned the body in the bush and returned
empty-handed. Although they had betrayed a trust,
they felt they had few choices. And once locals learned
the reason for the murders, they agreed to keep
their peace.' 'What was that reason?' asked Henry Harte;
but the farmer would not say. 'I might lose some sleep
if I told you,' he said. 'But I've got to the part
which you boys should find interesting. It is said
that, to this day, if you're staying in Howitt Hut
on a certain night, you cannot get into bed
without hearing moans and a repetitive thud
like someone stacking wood.' 'I don't believe in ghosts,'
said Henry Harte; but even the farmer could see
that he was enthralled. Yet what was uppermost
in our thoughts was the one piece of knowledge which he
had kept from us. Given that the killer's motive
could unlock the doorway his discretion had seemed
to close on, the farmer knew it in excessive
detail; and he looked wizened enough to have gleaned
his tale at first hand. Could he have been the young man
who discovered Bamford's body? He recounted
that part of his story with greater passion than
the rest, Henry Harte thought, and would have confronted
him with this suspicion had we not dissuaded
the notion. By this time we were on our way back
to the barn, which was striped in the moonlight, shaded
by cypress branches. Inside, it was coffin-black.

3.

Morning. Campfire smoke blown sideways among the trees.
A blackened jam tin with a wire handle, bubbling
on pine-cone embers. And Henry Harte on his knees,
stirring the tin with a stick: it was still troubling
to him that his response to the farmer's story

had come in conflict with his habitual style
as a hard-nosed doubter. The barn's inventory
of someone else's life would, in a little while,
be consumed by fire, but first we went over it.
The papers were meaningless to us, and the books
of little interest, and the clothes did not fit;
but then Gerald opened an envelope. 'This looks
promising,' he observed. 'It could be worth something
to an antique dealer or library some day.'
Yet when he showed it to me, I found the writing
difficult to read, with loops and curlicues, stray
points and slapdash crosses. The farmer had told us
we could keep anything which attracted our eye,
knowing we would have to hoist it on our shoulders
to take our selection away. We would not try
weighting our rucksacks down with china or steel, while
even paper could soon add pounds to our burden.
In the end we decided to take from the pile
just two letters each, which were chosen at random.
The rest heaped up outside the barn, a flammable mound
of paper, moth-holed clothes and damaged furniture.
We put a match to it, then sat down on the ground
to watch the fire take hold. Like a living creature
it was tentative at first, seeking out the ways
of weak resistance, recruiting tinder paper
and tender splinters, before returning to blaze
through those dissenting planks and table legs, vapour
of compelling force. Thin fingers of flame would leaf
through the pages of a book, idly, like someone
browsing, before dismissing its presence with brief
contempt. For Gerald the bonfire seemed to summon
a supernatural vision of demonic
power, though all it suggested to Henry Harte
was the rational action of economic
process. As the flames burned lower, we had to start
packing up. We would look at our letters later,
when we had time. With rucksacks on our backs, we knocked
at the farmhouse door. An old refrigerator
hummed away as we waited beside the unlocked
flyscreen. No one was home, it seemed. We might have left
our host unthanked, had we not met him on the road
outside, between two queues of poplars. 'Did you shift
all that stuff?' he asked us, and Gerald reassured

him that the job was complete. 'I've been out seeing
to that cow,' he said. 'She's walking around, all right,
but I wanted to find a calf that I could bring
for her to suckle. I hope you slept well, last night.'
The corners of his eyes creased upward as he made
this last enquiry. After conventional thanks
we went on our way, and at the day's end we stayed
on the river flats not far from our school. The banks
were covered with small yellow flowers, and waist-deep
bracken, and the icy river tumbled over
stones, swollen with melting snow. We now had to sleep
in our tents, without the luxurious cover
of the barn's wooden rafters. It was Sunday night
when we got back to the school, and then there were tests
and chores to be done, and the strange uplifting sight
of a chapel with a skillion roof; the rest
of the term slipped away, and the letters remained
unread. I put mine in the drawer where I kept
old bits of string and paperclips and pins, constrained
by some instinct from disposing of them. Time crept
over me. My schooldays had passed, and the letters
were still in the drawer, with keys and rolls of tape
and broken pens. Work came then, and next a better
job, and marriage, and days in the sun, as the shape
that my life would take emerged from pavilion
shadows. There was travel, and a change of city,
misplaced enthusiasms, and in due course children,
while the letters waited for me. And then thirty
years had gone by, and I was yet to get around
to finding out what they might be worth. The clutter
in my drawer was taking over, so I found
myself one day having to cull it. The utter
pointlessness of the hoarded treasures astonished
me: the perished rubber bands and unworn cuff-links,
the spools and cough-drop tins and the never-polished
blade of a never-used sword-shaped thing meant, I think,
for stirring cocktails; all had to go. And then there
were those letters. Before I threw them out, I had
to read them. The first did not take long: a mother
wrote to her son in the blandest terms; what she said
was unredeemed by its eighty-year-old post-date.
The second letter had come from Philadelphia,
and had more life. The writer's name was Rick McQuade.

The farmer's address was on the envelope. *Dear
Bob*, the letter began. *It seems like ages since
I had a line from you.* The year was twenty-one.
The paper had discoloured patches, like a quince
left in the air, but it wasn't as hard to read on
as I'd expected. *According to all reports
Aussie seems to be in a fairly bad condition
both as to crops and as to finance. Well, old sport,
over here its just the same. The country has been
awfully dry and only in the last few days
have we had any rain at all for about 40
days.* The repetitions were quite touching. *Today
however it is raining, just what the country
needs, a slow but sound rain. Business here is slack
but is picking up slowly but surely. Well, Bob,
as I'm sure you know I'm wishing I could come back
but it's best to wait while the fuss about that job
has died right down.* What could that reference mean? He
then changed the subject abruptly. *I guess you are
interested in the big fight that's not many
days off for the world's championship, aren't you? So far
as two weeks ago over a million dollars
worth of tickets had been sold. Great favor is thrust
upon Carpentier because he went to the war
and Dempsey did not. Well so much for the fight. I just
read in the papers that in one of the western
states a whole army of locusts, twenty miles long,
is eating up everything in sight. It's less than
rare. They have these hordes regularly, just as strong.
Well. The American Polo players made it
even against the English by winning hands down.*
Did the writer hope that something was evaded
through these digressions? *I will be going to town
after summer vacation. Conditions are awful
over here as regards to labor. Three million
men are out of work; it looks like many more will
be in the same pickle before too long. Civilian
life is enjoyable, I don't think. Well, I must
close now as I haven't any more to say. Don't
forget to write. You've not said anything, I trust,
about Wonnangatta. As you know, my wife won't
forgive me, though I thought it was for her honor
that I did what had to be done. So much for all*

of that. If anyone finds out I'm a goner.
The last words had been added in a hasty scrawl;
as I deciphered them it suddenly struck home
that I'd solved the murder mystery from all those
years ago. But of course it was too late. The chrome-
buffed fittings on a car parked outside my windows
reflected the afternoon sun in such a way
that a spectral outline, formed by a screen of leaves,
moved on the wall beside me. The climate today
leaves us no time for ghosts; only a child believes
in their existence. Yet after my daughter broke
my spectacles, I saw a fellow who'd been dead
for a fortnight walking toward me while I spoke
with someone in the street. I craned and turned my head
and saw, after all, it was not he, once the ghost
had come into the range of my focus. It struck
me then that these phantom visitations, almost
without exception, were seen in the time before we took
such forward strides in optometry and lighting
as to ensure that we see the world as it is.
Ghosts are confined to cartoons, no longer frightening.
We are rational, these days, unsuperstitious,
and all we have left to fear is within ourselves.
Perhaps it was always thus, but people once felt
differently. If the notion of fairies and wood-elves
is just childish, a human form able to melt
from view, transparent as a curtain or a veil,
excites the mind as do few other myths. We miss
such apparitions, now that the supernatural
has been ruled out. So it is easy to dismiss
the farmer's story with a stiff draught of logic:
what the cattleman saw must have been an effect
of moonlight among twisted snowgum limbs, a trick
that a passing cloud would soon dispel; or connect
him with the murders, for he knew where the body
was concealed. Yet such a dismissal leaves a bitter
taste, as Henry Harte found, I recalled, so many
years before. Had we paused to look at the letter
his sceptical thoughts would doubtless have been confirmed,
but the story would at once have lost its power.
A tale of murder with a neat solution, all trimmed
and rounded off, can still entertain us, but our
minds retain the unexplained for longer. Although

I realise, now, that it could not be the truth,
the farmer's version is what I prefer: the snow
still clinging in patches to the side of the roof
which angled away from the sun, and in the lee
of lichen-mottled boulders; the crouching, wind-fluked
snowgums; and the wash of moonlight in which, clearly
as a photograph, a man is raising a crooked
right hand. I put the letter back into the drawer.
Looking round, I glimpsed the sun's rays in a treetop
like a candle flame. The light stretched over the floor
in a band no wider than a folded envelope.

Social Behaviour of Minted Peas

Contradicting a proverb, the pot
I am watching boils, and resembles
the pool beneath a waterfall.
Then I pour in the frozen peas,
an avalanche of green stones, and at
that the pan no longer trembles.
For a while the peas lie as still
as the stony floor of the sea,
or else like a mountain of skulls
in South East Asia; they wait as
rigidly as an audience
with numbered seats, afraid to move.
Then one pea, on an odd impulse,
breaks away, and, with a skater's
motion from side to side, ascends
to ride the surface far above
the others, a non-conformist
with a notion all its own.
Another, hesitant at first, glides
up to join it, and others still,
one at a time, cannot resist
the temptation to follow on,

behind the first one who derides
the common and conventional.
And then it is clear there's a trend,
and all those peas who had hung back
now clamour to be allowed in.
Anxiously they jostle and sprint,
needing to belong in the end
among the upward-mobile pack,
elbowing each other, crowding
up to the air which smells of mint.

The Parapet

In their late nineties, both my grandmothers
reached a stage where death would be a relief,
at least to their relatives. Rather than grief
came a series of comic scenes others
may have found less amusing. Each woman,
long widowed, became senile, losing her human

faculties gradually, in the way
a painting might fade in the sunlight, or
plaster grow patchy with rising water.
The condition they had is known today
by a technical term, though one never
knows whether 'Alzheimer' is just a clever

American joke, or a real doctor's
name. My father's mother gave the first sign,
inadvertently, of her mind's decline,
when she enclosed with one of her letters
a scrap of paper on which her hand, grown
shaky, had scribbled fragments she'd have known

in childhood: the refrain from some old poem,
and excerpts of long-lost nursery rhymes.
The letter itself was, as at other times,
measured and sensible, the blue script firm
and upright, but that careless enclosure
showed what lay beneath her manner of sure

civility: in her mind she resembled
someone sliding off a cliff, and scrambling
for a hand-hold. Her letters grew rambling,
after this, and her handwriting jumbled.
Reports came back from my father's sisters,
who were living nearby, and whose assistance

came to be indispensable. At first
she was just forgetful, but then she grew
so confused that it seemed she hardly knew
who anyone was. She had to be nursed
day and night. Having slipped from the precipice
her mind had tried to cling onto, she was

in slow-motion flight towards the crevasse
we know to be bottomless. She became
a mischievous child, whose favourite game
was to make escapes. On the green terrace
of lawns which sloped down from her hilltop house
she would wander aimless and on the loose,

until the day when she had gone missing
and panic reigned for hours. At last a phone
call came: she had made her way on her own,
by train and taxi, to one of the city
department stores, intending, so she said,
to do some shopping, except that her head,

when she got there, became like a building
site emptied in an enemy air-raid.
She could not remember, or had mislaid,
what she had come for, and the store's gilding
on pillars and shopfittings had increased
her confusion; nor did she have the least

idea where she had come from. The call
was made by a store detective who found
her acting strangely. She was guarded round
the clock after that, but soon despite all
her nurses' watchfulness she disappeared
again. They searched all day, and this time feared

the worst. Then someone looking for a torch
went into the garage, where an as-new
black Daimler, up on blocks, had been unused
since she grew too old for it: a side porch
led into there, though the main garage door
was locked, and Grandmother was in the car,

holding onto the wheel, pretending to drive.
In my other grandmother, the effect
of age was to enhance every defect
while erasing virtues which help one survive
in society. Where her snobbery
had once been veiled by a feathery

layer of politeness, it now remained
like a rock exposed at low tide: the gull
which once perched on that rock had flown her skull.
Patience, affection and kindness were drained
away, and the residue left behind
had a bitter taste. That she be confined

to a nursing home seemed unavoidable,
though it did nothing for her. She'd telephone
my mother every day, who came in person
daily. Once she complained, 'There's a horrible
man in my room, and he won't go away.'
Alarmed, my mother hurried all the way

back to the vine-surrounded hospice bed
where all her mother faced was a TV
set. Another time, 'You never visit me,'
was the accusation; but then she said:
'Who is that dreadful woman who comes in
every day?' The sweet scent of jasmine

blew under her room's window-lintel,
yet it might have been a prison cell for all
her pleasure with it. A familial
event, about the time when their mental
state was weakest, brought my two grandmothers
to pose in a photograph together,

along with the other guests at the wedding.
Though their smiles looked vague, the camera's eye
could not disclose what everyone, and I,
knew of their lives – the nights on soiled bedding,
and days of drifting like a white-haired ghost.
It seemed to me what both of them had lost

was a portion of the soul, and on that
I started brooding: was it feasible
for one's spirit to become immortal
in a piecemeal fashion, one facet at
a time? Could the nobility of one
grandmother, and the other's sweetness, come

back and be restored in an afterworld?
I thought it, at the least, improbable,
the mind and soul being indivisible,
for the soul to be gradually furled
away and then reassembled elsewhere,
like the cottage in the park whose bricks were

numbered and shipped over twelve thousand miles.
Such far-fetched notions could not be canvassed
seriously, yet without them I faced
the knowledge that we were machines: our smiles
and tears and night-time terrors were nothing
more than the reactions of a breathing

chemical chain. The body could survive,
it seemed, the extinction of its soul,
but if that were so we could not be whole
in the way I had thought of it. To live
on, as my grandmothers had, as a shell
of the self felt worse than the threat of hell,

and much more real. Seeing them both became,
for me, a vertiginous torture, like
hanging off the parapet of the spike-
topped tower at my school, causing the same
blank panic in the mind. That parapet
afforded a vista over carpet-

smooth fields and hedges, and over the roofs
of red-brick buildings, but the imagined
fall I now peered into would never end,
and could not be conceived in all its truth.
My grandmothers both deserved sympathy;
instead I was lost in youth's self-pity.

We dread death less as we grow closer to it.
The qualms which absorbed me then are the province,
nearly, of anybody's adolescence;
when they linger further in one's life, though, it
can mean that black depression, another
newly named complaint, has come to smother

one. Yet for the rest of the family
my grandmothers' senility had meant
that the pain which must come with bereavement
had been spread out, as if paid easily
through an instalment plan, one that matured
on the day of each funeral. Adjured

to attend, I declined, citing prior
arrangements which were not true, and then shame
consumed me for days. Now I think the blame
was undeserved: fearing to climb higher
up the mind's parapet we should refuse
if sanity depends from how we choose.

Rage

Anger only serves
to aggravate the hurt
inflicted by the first
injustice done to us;

yet who could feel no rage
in the face of a barrage
purposefully charged
with provocation as

a disobedient child
or someone who reviles
the essence of our style
in a tone of careless

malice? Those who give way
to anger find people shy
from them, almost as if they
had become the reverse

of a magnetic pole,
but so long as we still
believe our dismissal
unjust, or a bruise

unfairly given,
the pain will return
with efforts to maintain
our fury over those

unhealing injuries.
Often those who are angry
appear to have their way,
but at a cost which is

more than any expects.
Rage is like that: it's
something no one forgets.
And no one else forgives.

Mon Père Est Mort

For an oral exam, when aged thirteen,
my father was asked questions in French
by a visiting professor in trench-
coat and gold-rimmed spectacles, who was lean

with the thin, pursed lips of an enemy
interrogator. He pressed my father
to say what his father's *métier*
was – an awkward question, for how many

schoolboys know the French for 'Real Estate
Agent'? Adopting a tragic expression,
my father just replied *'Mon père est mort.'*

The professor blushed to commiserate;
when the results of the examination
were known, my father had the highest score.

Summer Traffic Jam

Held in the traffic, his car hemmed in by the heat,
he notices that every lane and driveway,
each garage entrance and side street, seems to secrete
more cars, like shining beads of sweat. It is the day

of the appointment which must reverse a decline
in his life, and his mind has transformed the city's
road system into pores. Time leaks away in fine
portions, relentless as traffic fines. For pity's

sake, he prays, let this knot be untied. The idling
engine of a shed-sized van, which stands alongside
the open window where his elbow keeps sidling
away from the sun's shifting griller flame, seems applied

as a torturer's ratchet, to increase his pain.
The rumbling of a truck adds another degree,
as does any source of noise. An aeroplane
booms overhead, and road drills hammer hotly.

A bus, a spinning tyre, and even a car's
radio all work to swell the temperature.
The sun is present everywhere, in points like stars
which glare off this detail and that chrome aperture

directly toward his eyes, as if a merciless
interrogator were focussing a desk lamp
from the car bumpers, windscreens, wheel-trims and wireless
aerials which construct his prison walls. The damp

clothes creep on his skin. On a shop awning a clock
displays the time, which at first may have oozed like sweat
before he felt the moments building, block by block,
with him still unable to move. Growing like debt,

the minutes keep adding more floors to mountain-size
towers of lateness which mount up in his mind,
until he dreams of ascending one such high-rise
to leap, and launch his despair on the sleep-warm wind.

The Childhood Charter

That which is forbidden or refused us is what we most urgently
desire.

What we are given freely, for our good, is to be viewed with
suspicion and usually rejected.

We cry for More, unless More is available, in which case we want
less.

Cleanliness does not interest us.

The possessions of others appeal to us more than our own.

We appreciate the notion of sharing, but believe it should not be practised by us.

We sleep and wake at inconvenient hours.

It exhilarates us to flee from our protection, until out of its reach, whereat terror engulfs us.

Our deepest fears are of what we do not know, yet the unknown lures us irresistibly.

We know more than anyone can guess, but less than we would like to.

Although we expect to be obeyed, we do not practise obedience.

We talk, and interrupt, continually, ceaseless as a bubbling spring, until asked to say something, whereupon all our words run dry.

Failure enrages us, and we brazenly flaunt our triumphs.

Achieving our greatest desire renders it worthless.

We could not be more self-centred, nor more dependent on people outside our selves.

Though we feel we are held captive by our protectors, in fact we are their captors.

When three of us are gathered together, we conspire against the third.

We expect love from everyone we meet, but the ones we prefer are those who refuse us love.

Some of us never cease to be children.

Mullet Leap

Summer was a haze of midges
over the lake, and the hired canoe's bow
    pushed through reflected images
of sand hills and mangrove thickets. For now

    the world was at peace. Dragonflies
hovered like miniature helicopters
    escorting a warship the size
of a tin bathtub; the insects' copper

    green scales gleamed in a dream-clear light.
Half-noticed out of one eye, I thought that
    a silver bottle crossed my sight
to splash down into the canoe's wide, flat

    wake. What was happening? Who could
have flung a bottle from the shore? It seemed
    unpopulated. I understood
when a shining fish leapt where midges teemed

    beside me, to fall back after
gulping down a near-invisible
    mouthful. Paddling my craft or
resting, I watched out for more. A bubble

    would appear now and then, and once
it seemed there was a splash behind my back,
    but that was all. One fleeting glance
of silver had awoken a new lack

    in my life, because now I longed
to glimpse such a fish again. In my mind
    it grew dimensions, rainbow-thonged
behind its gills, detailed and then refined

    in perfect scale: could it be river
trout, or Atlantic salmon, some species
    I had read about but never
encountered? Yet the only breed found in these

tide-filled lakes was the common grey
mullet, which was all that crossed the bow
    of the plywood canoe that day,
though the aquarium standing somehow

    inside my head had space for all
manner of specimens to leap and swim.
    Dragonflies hovered in the tall
heat. The afternoon light began to dim

    as the shadow of a sand hill
edged across the lake. A voice called out from
    the boathouse – my time was up. Still
I kept on waiting for more fish to come.

    And would wait for years. Only when
returning as an adult to the lake shore
    would my longing be resolved. Then,
strolling where mangrove swamp had been before

    developers came to carve out
a golf course, I heard the same sound and saw
    the mullet leap until all doubt
had been erased. They became familiar

    as the gaping fin-sharp display
one finds in the fish-shop window, passing
    down the street every other day.
And now perhaps something else was missing.

Relativity

Here is a question where measurement fails,
though not quantum theory, maybe –
a crying baby weighs more than a sleeping baby,
yet it doesn't show on the scales.

The Salute

At a beach near peaceful Cape Town
as the war's storm raged around,
a Catalina crouched at anchor,
awkward as a crippled swan.

The flying boat's Australian aircrew
swimming unclothed in the bay
saw a thunderstorm approaching,
knew that when it blew their way

the plane would be capsized and sunk,
knew that there was nothing they could
do but take off from the swell.
No time to dress. The squadron leader

swam out to the mooring-buoy
and swarmed aboard. Lightning-strikes
lit up the sky like tracer fire.
The engines, loud as motorbikes,

began to roar, before the plane
lumbered off the deep green waves
and climbed. A shelf of clouds
dank as walls in limestone caves

loomed up ahead. The pilot turned
and hugged the eastward-bearing coast
toward the nearest airforce base
a hundred miles away. With tanks almost

dry, he cleared the storm and found
the harbour he was looking for,
then taxied in, and moored the plane.
He dived and swam toward the shore,

marched up a beach and through a gate
– still in the nude – by guards who looked
up open-mouthed as he went on
past the mess where airmen cooked

last meals for other airmen who
would soon fly off to cruise the lanes
of shipping in the U-boat-prowled
linked oceans which embrace the Cape. Lines

of doors ajar in passageways
led him through an office block
where the adjutant, at his desk,
glanced up from some paperwork,

a stack of files and documents
and orders he was executing:
on the carpet there before him
stood a naked man, saluting.

Getting a Girl into Bed

Did any Lothario
struggling to undress a girl
with her connivance
(disguised as coy resistance)
confront such an obstacle
as that posed by a four-year-old

who won't undress for the bath?
It was easier for Don Juan
to get a girl into bed
putting false ideas in her head
than to cross the bear-strewn,
doll-and-toy-cluttered path

to lure a child to sleep; yet had he guessed
the routines which would fill his life
if the sheep's membrane failed
him – voices which wailed
all night, a surly wife –
would he be impressed?

Such a fate is what Casanova fears,
of course, and takes pain
to avoid. Yet who is to measure
a fleeting pleasure
against what there is to gain,
having it in one's power to end those tears?

Electric Razor

My worn electric razor – twenty years
    old – looked a bit like a coffin,
or else like one of the motor cars
of its vintage, a family sedan,

perhaps, designed with sparse adornment,
    a black box with a metal grille
at one end. It performed the task meant
for it well enough, although it did feel,

when I touched my jaw, that my shaven skin
    had the texture of sandpaper:
snaps taken at the time made me appear in
shadow. If I cleaned the razor, black pepper

would be sprinkled over the bathroom sink
    as I unclipped the cutter's lid –
remnants of bristles, I used to think,
which resembled iron filings. They made

me think, also, about time's passing,
    and the way the body's surface
grew another layer, discarding
one every night, and printed the mattress

with a record detailed as tree-rings.
    Such notions are, to say the least,
disquieting, a habit of mind one longs
to leave behind. As the years drifted past

it seemed I might, as the morning shave became
    a mindless routine. Then l got
myself a swivel-head razor. At home,
unpacked from its soft fake leather wallet,

it had the lines of a sports car, narrow
    and streamlined, and weighed as little
as the device in a terrorist's hollow
suitcase lid, though it was safe as a child's rattle

or a cellular telephone. When I
    used it, the painless electric
massage made my skin feel as if newly
reborn. Instead of a square metal rack

over the cutting blades, there was a curved
    and delicate fine-laced cover
like the cowling on a jet engine, carved
out of paper-thin steel, and whenever

I shaved it felt like being in control
    of a speeding war-plane. One day,
following the instruction booklet as well
as I could, I decided at last to try

and clean the 'cutter block' described in its
    ambiguous language. Released
from the cowling, a heap of trimmed offcuts
spilled over the window-sill like the dust

from a vacuum cleaner. In the clear light
    that pile resembled the ashes
a person is reduced to in the heat
of a crematorium, nails, eyelashes

and all. The greyness showed to me, as well,
    that the day was getting nearer
whereon I would become such a small pile
of ash, kept in a mantelpiece urn, or far

from here, beneath some cemetery's lawns
    – green and regularly mown – where light
spills across the brass plaques fixed to headstones
while unfamiliar cars pass slowly down the street.

A Game of Dominoes

Indian summer steams among the thickets
of bamboo and overgrown shrubs, outside
the abandoned church, where broken pickets
dangle on the fence, and three men sit wild-eyed

on a wooden bench. Unkempt, with matted hair,
they have shabby coats with brown-paper-wrapped
bottles in each pocket, and trousers stained where
zippers yawn apart. One feels they are trapped

in a life where every hope stumbles
into another obstacle or dead
end, and thus that the derelict churchyard mocks

at their fate. Passing, one expects mumbles
and liquor smells and blank stares; the three, instead,
calmly play dominoes on an upturned box.

Swear Words

Enraged when I refuse
to let her harm herself
by falling off a table,
my two-year-old's abuse
consists of expressions
she must have overheard
without being able
to grasp their intentions:

'You bigwig!' she exclaims.
'You copycat!' Accustomed,
like everybody else,
to being given names
by drivers in traffic
jams, or bad-tempered wives
in supermarket aisles,
these words are less graphic,

of course, than the curses
one hears in the outside
world, yet their intended
meaning, on the surface,
is the same. From now on
when anybody swears
I'll not be offended;
the rough tongues of workmen,

bartenders and drunkards,
police and criminals,
can utter nothing new.
I recognise their words
as being only that
invective of a child,
not (blank) and (blank), but, 'You
bigwig! You copycat!'

A Royal Pardon

Sir Gilbert Eliott of Stobs,
my distant ancestor, was known
for his temper. One of the clubs
    in the border town

of Jedburgh to which he belonged
had recorded an incident
in its annals where, feeling wronged
    in an argument

with his neighbour, Mr Stewart,
he had drawn his sword and thrust it
through the man's torso; he withdrew it
    only when his trusted

butler, witnessing the fight,
took hold of his arm. Both he
and Stewart had drunk deeply that night,
    and Sir Gilbert's eye

was glazed; he remained in his chair,
unseeing, while his victim slumped
mortally hurt on the floor.
    The servant's hand thumped

Sir Gilbert to awaken him,
for he saw his master's peril
from Stewart's friends; had taken him,
    then, like a barrel

slung over his back, from the room,
downstairs, and into a graveyard
nearby; and placed him on a tomb
    covered with a plaid

for concealment, while Sir Gilbert
slept. Only when his employer
awoke could a desperate
    plight be faced with sober

recognition. Ever-faithful,
the butler arranged an escape
to France, where Sir Gilbert's exile
    lasted two years. Drapes

covered the furniture at the house
in Stobs. Some friends remained loyal,
despite mutterings and rumours.
    And then a royal

pardon was devised; Sir Gilbert's
petition reached the king, who conferred,
in due course, for cutting Stewart's
    garment with his sword,

the sovereign forgiveness. No mention
of what injury was caused, beneath
the sword-torn cloak. On his return,
    refreshed in health,

to Scotland, Sir Gilbert lived
on into ripe age, did not earn
any further enemies, contrived
    no further action

to affront the peace, got married,
and fathered four boys. His grandson
became a baronet, who was buried
    at Westminster; one

of *his* grandsons, in turn, then sired
an adventurous youth who sailed
to Botany Bay, and retired,
    years later, availed

of the generous pension paid
to magistrates in Queensland.
The map of descendants would spread
    in a widening band

like blood on the floor of the room
upstairs at the Black Bull inn
where Sir Gilbert dined. For him
    killing was less a sin

than an inconvenient mishap.
Living at the edge of the stain
I dread becoming the kind of chap
    to do all that again.

Don't Laugh at Girls

Frustrated again! When I forbid
her clean boots from straying into mud
the fury of my daughter
reduces me to laughter.
Her two-year-old forehead curls:
'Don't laugh at girls!'

Another time, 'Girls wear dresses,'
is a rule she espouses.
The tone of voice makes clear
that nobody should dare
to call into question
an absolute equation.

'Sexism', I begin to feel, is not
society's construct,
nor is it devised to enforce
unfairly gender-slanted laws:
all it resembles is the view
of most children when aged two.

Colours, she has now decided,
are unchangeably divided
into sex-roles, 'girl' and 'boy',
and likewise every kind of toy
is assigned to one of them.
Clinging to her mother's hem,

she holds forth on principles
which decide the place of 'girls',
and define the extramural.
Always in the plural,
'girls' is what she calls herself,
as though an inner wealth

permitted her to stand for all
the sex. Along the wall
white flowers bloomed beside our kitchen
until she climbed up high to pick them.
Guilty, standing on a chair,
she's defiant: 'Girls don't care.'

Glass on the Chimney

Irascible Mr Fell, who married
    my father's sister, provoked at least
        irritation in everyone he met,
    from waiters in dining-rooms to the priest
        at his wedding; his coarse manner would get
            the calmest souls harried
    and aggravated. His own family
        endured such behaviour as to make life
        a constant trial of patience; his wife
    suffered, in the way one did then, silently,

but left an eloquent understatement
　　with a diary she had been keeping
　　　　throughout her teenage years. I came to read
　　what my aunt wrote because I had been sleeping
　　　　at her daughter's house – she'd
　　　　　　opened out the parchment
　　pages of a soft vellum-bound volume
　　　　which had passed to her upon her mother's
　　　　death. Her inheritance comprised, other
　　than the diary and some small heirloom,

only her father's temper, which she used
　　for ends she hoped he would have disapproved.
　　　　As a diarist, my aunt was fluent
　　and always cheerful, someone who loved
　　　　to record the detail of innocent
　　　　　　events which had amused
　　her, parties and picnic outings, flowers
　　　　she had nurtured in her garden, the beach
　　　　in summer, and winters huddled in reach
　　of a blazing log fire; inscribing the hours

leading up to her marriage, the bright tone
　　was unchanged, until one final entry:
　　　　John means well, of course, but some days I fear
　　　　we don't understand each other. The diary
　　　　　　pages henceforward were left blank, as year
　　　　　　succeeded year. The stone
　　mask which her face became, in middle age,
　　　　was carved, I could see, by all that remained
　　　　unwritten. My cousin was not restrained
　　by her upbringing, for, when she got engaged

to a suitably qualified young man,
　　her pleased father loudly let it be known
　　　　that one of the conditions in his will
　　prescribed that both of his daughters, when grown,
　　　　should marry to inherit his wealth. And still,
　　　　　　after the final span
　　of his days, there was a fortune to be shared
　　　　by his heirs. My cousin, the younger
　　　　of the sisters, reacted with anger:
　　she cancelled all her wedding plans, and hired

a compliant surgeon who agreed to tie
     the fallopians, leaving her sterile;
          she then became an early supporter
of feminism and other radical
          causes. Her sister, the dutiful daughter,
               would not allow their line to die
along with the name, and married twice instead,
          earning a double share of the estate
          in the most literal way. The burning hate
my cousin felt when their father was dead

and her wealthy sister called with complaints
     about the expenses which were involved
          in maintaining the airconditioners
at her new holiday home, at last devolved
          to become one of those simmering fevers
               which motivate both saints
and idealists, as well as the criminal.
          Reduced to dwelling in a damp hovel,
          like a character from someone's novel,
my radical cousin survived with minimal

comforts. The book-piled study – it was little
     more than a shed – which accommodated
          me had also harboured activists
on the run from the police; a celebrated
          aboriginal, opposed to the racists'
               law, slept for several
months where I stayed just two days. Her father,
     who was alive then, had business dealings
     in Southern Africa, so her feelings
on the question of race had a rather

vengeful edge. Yet no revenge on Mr Fell
     surpassed that of the builder who was hired
          to construct a mansion for him. After
months of aggravation, he was inspired,
          the builder, bullied from floor to rafter
               till he could barely quell
the impulse to reply with an equal
          measure, to devise a stealthy payback
          for his torment. Atop the chimney-stack
at the centre of the great house, a final

row of brickwork awaited a finishing trim:
the builder climbed up, and, when unobserved,
fixed a pane of glass above the chimney.
It was the least that his client deserved.
Mr Fell moved into the house, and when he
lit fires, smoke followed him
around the room. Thinking still-green firewood
was to blame, or the wind, he only saw
that he could not get the chimney to draw.
Cold winters were to pass before he understood.

Lawnmower Sestina

'the act of mowing a lawn is spiritually depleting'
— Murray Bail

Most complaint is boasting in disguise:
this maxim shapes itself in my mind
while I propel the motor-mower
in circles round that corner of the lawn
where the outdoor table stands upon a square
of brickwork. Who would suspect the pleasure

in this circular routine, such pleasure
that, I'm told, my expression can't disguise
a silent exultation as the lawn
is transformed by the action of the mower,
its surface made as even as the square,
as repetition works to smooth the mind.

It is exertion which I do not mind,
entailing the particular pleasure
craftsmen and artists feel. To carve a square
of carpet-like soft grass, where the lawn
is sheltered by a trellis for disguise
from next door's terrace, the spinning mower

becomes something other, not a mower
but a painter's green brushstrokes, in my mind.
The work of art which prompts this pleasure
levels overgrown grassblades to disguise
their nature; it is like rounding a square,
civilising herbage into a lawn.

Walking on it, I know it is my lawn,
Just as the house is mine, and the mower,
and that knowledge, I see, is the pleasure
householders are attempting to disguise
as they bemoan a task no one should mind
performing. The window frames are square

and painted green; reflected in each square
is a vision of the newly shaven lawn.
My spirit, as I mow, or my mind,
fills up, as does the bin behind the mower
which catches all the clippings, with pleasure
like a mound of trimmed-off grass. A disguise

for that pleasure, which remains when the mower
has returned to its square green shed, the lawn
fragrant under the sun, in the mind is no disguise.

Moving Time

The house was too small; it was time to move from it,
and doubts began about the neighbourhood
after a red-faced man had paused to vomit

against the parking sign outside. Omit
the harbour breezes and amenities – one could
see it was too small. It was time to move from it.

Hearing the car-alarms night after night emit
a squeal like that of chainsaws jammed in wood,
and noticing a drug-abuser pause to vomit

in the gutter where the cars were parked, the comfort
of the light-filled bedroom seemed the only good
about the house. It was time to move from it.

A little man at the gate called 'Hellooo Comet',
delivering an unrequested package. He stood
astride a pond of alcoholic vomit

where last night's rugby followers reached the summit
of their drinking song. How else to conclude
but that the time had come to move from it,
and from the passers-by who paused to vomit?